# English
# and
# Reading
# in a
# Changing
# World

## Edited by Eldonna L. Evertts
## University of Illinois

## National Council of Teachers of English

CONSULTANT READERS FOR THIS MANUSCRIPT

Gilbert M. Gravelle, Minocqua Elementary School, Wisconsin
Richard Lloyd-Jones, University of Iowa
Ruth Reeves, Houston Independent School District, Texas

NCTE COMMITTEE ON PUBLICATIONS

Robert F. Hogan, Chairman, NCTE Executive Secretary
Robert Dykstra, University of Minnesota
Walker Gibson, University of Massachusetts, Amherst
Robert E. Palazzi, Burlingame High School, California
Eugene C. Ross, NCTE Director of Publications

EDITORIAL SERVICES    Linda Jeanne Reed, NCTE Headquarters

BOOK DESIGN    Norma Phillips Meyers, NCTE Headquarters

Library of Congress Catalog Card Number LC 78-171578
ISBN 0-8141-0162-4
NCTE Stock Number 01624

# Contents

# Contents

# Introduction

## by Eldonna L. Evertts

The challenge in English and reading today is change—not just superficial rearrangement of outmoded content and practices, but thoroughgoing and purposeful change that goes to the roots of our subject. On the one hand, there is the evidence of changes needed now to help improve programs for children we have failed so far. Beyond that, there is the need to plan with an eye toward changes in teaching media and school organization—changes already underway and rapidly expanding.

The impact of the Anglo-American Seminar on the Teaching of English (the Dartmouth Seminar) upon current educational thought has made it necessary for educators to reevaluate current programs in the light both of the philosophy set forth at Dartmouth and of the support and criticism that philosophy has elicited. A successful, innovative program can come into being only if those planning the new program study, evaluate, and finally synthesize the thinking of scholars who represent a variety of positions.

*English and Reading in a Changing World* offers a broad base for presenting the thinking of outstanding researchers and scholars. These articles were drawn from papers read at a series of institutes cosponsored by the University of Illinois and the National Council of Teachers of English under a special NDEA grant from the United States Office of Education. The institutes for state supervisors of English and reading were held in Urbana, Illinois; Tallahassee, Florida; Austin, Texas; Seattle, Washington; and Sturbridge, Massachusetts. Each paper reflects elements of change in curriculum development and in the teaching of English.

The structure of this publication departs markedly from the usual division with such headings as literature, language, composition, and the language arts skills. Here, instead, the dominant themes are the humanity of English, creative literacy, verbal sequencing, literary responsiveness, and emerging language sensitivity. Consequently, these articles now speak to a much broader audience than the groups of state supervisors enrolled in the institutes. The classroom teacher, the local supervisor, the curriculum builder, the student of education and of English—all will be interested. It is urgent that all those currently responsible for English in schools and colleges consider the whole range of current thought on English, its role and function.

The topics in this collection are broadly conceived; there is no uniformity of opinion. Authors describe the content of English at preschool, elementary, secondary and college levels. Those authors who stress the importance of language in the field of English offer a variety of definitions of language study and views of creativity. Other writers stress the importance of literature even during the early educational years. In addition to theoretical discussions of language and literature, the monograph contains discussions of teacher education and a variety of practical applications. The grouping of papers here is by the stance of the speaker-authors toward this audience as well as by their messages.

Articles in the first group express the convictions underlying current efforts to center the teaching of English on individual creativity. Robert C. Pooley summarizes the Dartmouth Seminar, succinctly, yet completely, offering a framework for the consideration of many of the papers that follow. His focus is on the lessons to be learned from the meeting of British and American education specialists and scholars in the areas of speech, language, drama, writing, literature as experience, and teaching. He challenges the reader to develop more creative programs in the elementary and secondary schools, and in the colleges and universities.

Stanley B. Kegler offers one explanation of the meaning of English. He notes difficulties of describing its components and processes. The Dartmouth definition of English, he feels, is a description of what a child *does* as he learns through language, and therefore is a limited perception. He asks for a balance between the doctrine of utility and that of cultural values, and a balance between the language scholars and the teachers in our schools. If teaching is going to be purposeful, then teachers must help students resolve problems and become more effective human beings. Geoffrey Summerfield is also concerned with making the study of English more humane, especially the study of poetry. In his article "Some Ways into Poetry and with Poetry," he emphasizes the potential of an approach designed simply to encourage children to experience poetry. The teacher should select material a student can relate to personally and reject pedantic, authoritarian teaching. A community of attentiveness and responsiveness is the goal.

The second section consists of articles which focus on changes which have occurred in recent years in the approaches to the teaching of various aspects of English. Frank J. Zidonis believes that the vision of grammar has vastly expanded. Grammar is an attempt to explain, on the one hand, how we are able to form sentences almost effortlessly and, on the other, how one interprets or understands sentences. He suggests that a movement now exists to make semantics a greater concern in language study. His illustrations illuminate his argument for novices as well as for more sophisticated students. A different line of investigation into language is the one taken by Stanley M. Sapon. He prefers to call language "verbal behavior," a special way of behaving, not a "thing." He emphasizes the importance of looking at the function of language as well as the form. In conclusion he shows that, given the proper stimulus setting, stimulus control and occasion for emission of that behavior, the shape of verbal behavior at the preschool level can be the same as at the university level.

Paul S. Olson sets forth the premise that myths have four universal characteristics and that these elements are common to myths from Western civilization and from other cultures, and to the narratives children tell at school or at home. He draws on children's verbal creations to illustrate his discussion of myths.

Section three consists of surveys of current practices in the area of children's literature, reading at the elementary and secondary levels, composition at the elementary level, and a case study on curriculum planning. Related to these descriptions of current programs are references to non-grading, individualization of instruction computers, programmed learning, and other innovations.

William A. Jenkins explains how the children's book world,

including fiction, fact, and poetry, has now become a universe. Children's literature must not occupy an otherwise empty moment in the school day. It should become a vital component of the total school curriculum. While literature helps a pupil "to bring order and control to his life, it in turn is ordered and controlled by life." Reading is closely related to literature; the skill acquires significance when children engage in reading books. Yet, unless ample attention is given to the development of this skill, pupils never find the free, full enjoyment that can be theirs through literature. Other current practices in the teaching of reading are presented by William J. Iverson. He groups the new views of reading at the elementary level as changes in concepts of readiness, changes in materials and methods of instruction, changes in organization for instruction, and changes in means of evaluation. At the secondary level, Iverson would like to see more basic continuing instruction for the average reader, reading instruction in every subject, extended instruction for very able readers, and intensive instruction for retarded readers.

Alvina T. Burrows recognizes that computers can tell us much about language, but she believes our concern should be the creativity that both teachers and children can bring to the act of composing. She stresses the idea that "writing is a distinctly human affair done by people and for people."

J. Harlan Shores summarizes the current scene in curriculum development and reenforces the point that language-based models offer a potently successful basis for planning an English curriculum that is analogous to those developed in science and math. He isolates developments in curriculum most closely related to teaching communication: reselection of content with a view toward structure of subjects, care of deviant portions of the population, psychological aspects of communication, the technological revolution, and nongradedness.

In the final section, the articles concern the difficult and changing role of the teacher in the classroom. Edward H. Rosenheim discusses the need for teachers to follow a middle course, rather than develop a monolithic conception of literacy. He defines literacy as not a mastery of language, but a mastery of those areas of experience communicated through language. He pleads for creativity in the teaching of English, ". . . a 'making,' a shaping of comprehension and imagination and feeling into a unity which had not existed before."

An account of curriculum in San Diego is presented by Robert A. Bennett. He discusses ten steps to be followed in order to provide a balanced program of instruction, describing the reading program and the range of language, composition, and literature that is offered to students. Attention is called to the use of drama, improvisation, dialogue, and role-playing as advocated in the Dartmouth Seminar papers.

Michael F. Shugrue, in the concluding paper, discusses the tremendous impact the Dartmouth Seminar and the Project English Centers have had on curriculum planning, but he also emphasizes the need for extensive change in English classrooms. English teachers need new ideas and information in order to escape old methods of instruction. ". . . Supervisors must focus on the few activities which affect each English teacher every week in almost every class."

The editor hopes that the excitement engendered by a changing world, changing curricula, changing ideas and perhaps changing ideologies will stimulate readers to bring fresh thinking to their own areas of endeavor and encourage them to develop new approaches to fit the needs of their students.

E. Evertts

# The Role of Language
# in Promoting Individualism

## Part One

*We are addicted to grade placement and a rigid schedule of class hours of the same length and frequency for all students. Some subjects may possibly be taught superbly in this pattern, but I think no one will challenge me when I say that English is not one of them.*

# The Dartmouth Seminar and the Supervision of English

## by Robert C. Pooley

The subject of this address is the impact of the Dartmouth Seminar on the teaching of English and the special implications of the reports of that seminar upon the state-wide responsibility in the supervision of and curriculum building in the language arts. The term "language arts" includes all aspects of the English language in schools from the kindergarten through grade twelve, including speech, drama, journalism, and other specialties that employ the English language.

In late August and early September of 1966 a group of teachers and scholars, all concerned in one way or another with the teaching of English, assembled at Dartmouth College in Hanover, New Hampshire. Canada, Great Britain, and the United States were represented in the group.

**Dr. Robert C. Pooley**
Emeritus Professor of English
University of Wisconsin, Madison

As an outcome of this seminar two reports have been published, from which I have drawn the views in this paper. An American participant, Herbert J. Muller of Indiana University, has published a book entitled *The Uses of English,* which he calls "a report on the proceedings of the Seminar, designed for the general reader." [1] It is a practical book, with its focus on the classroom and the procedures therein which might achieve the goals set by the conference. A British participant, John Dixon of Bretton Hall, College of Education, Wakefield, England, has published *Growth through English,* of which he says,

> It has been my aim to draw from the discussions and reports at Dartmouth such ideas as are directly relevant to my own work in class and to that of teachers I know . . . . In taking from the dialogue of the Seminar what would help me make sense of English as I know it, my aim has been not to make an end of discussion (by a sort of super summing-up) but rather to propose a new starting point. [2]

In effect, Dixon's book is a professional guide to teachers, and Muller's is a popular treatment for teachers and the general reader.

In the applications I make of these reports to our work as state supervisors, I draw much of basic principle from Dixon and much of classroom practice from Muller. Nevertheless, these roles will be sometimes reversed, for Dixon speaks convincingly of classroom practice, and Muller presents principle and viewpoint with effective clarity.

I shall organize my remarks on the lessons to be learned from the Dartmouth Seminar in a series of topics related to the teaching of English and our leadership as supervisors. I begin with the question, "What is English?" What is it that we teach?

Early in the Seminar, by general consensus, the effort to define English specifically was dropped. Because of wide divergencies of view it appeared better to ask what English does, or can do. Muller summarizes thus:

> It is a commonplace that democracy more than any other kind of society needs literate, informed, critical citizens. If it is not absolutely essential that they be able to write well, it is desirable that they be able to speak well, and certainly important that they be able to read and listen well. One way of sizing up the English curriculum—in both the schools and the colleges—is to ask how well it is serving this basic purpose, which no other subject attends to directly. Another way is to ask how well designed it is to instill a respect for, and to

develop powers of discrimination in, the civilized human values that democracy attempts to make available to all its citizens.[3]

I would interpret this to mean that English is the subject whose purpose is to enable citizens of a democracy to communicate with each other at the best possible level of understanding; and that it is concerned with human values, treated with respect, and critically appraised. In curriculum writing, in teacher training, and in supervisory guidance we could properly ask the question about every proposal of method and material: does it advance effectively the process of communication in a setting of respect and critical appraisal of human values? If we can't say what English is, we might some day be able to say that these things are what English does.

## Talking

Dixon says,

> . . . members of the Seminar noted that some of us referred to "talk" in class, others to "speech". . . . "Talk" tends to be used of less formal occasions . . . "speech" implies accent or pronunciation . . . "classroom talk" may then be used as the generic term. . . . "Speech" seems to be rarely used today for verbal interaction, whereas we do say "we talked about it, talked it over, had a heart to heart talk." [4]

You will note the key phrase in this quotation, "verbal interaction." Dixon is making the point that in what is labeled "speech" this verbal interaction may not occur at all. Yet it is the very heart of language experience. He sums up,

> . . . language is learnt in operation, not by dummy runs. In English, pupils meet to share their encounters with life, and to do this effectively they move freely between dialogue and monologue—between talk, drama, and writing; and literature, by bringing new voices into the classroom, adds to the store of shared experience.[5]

Contrast this summary with the usual outline of a speech course and you will see at once why the Seminar emphasizes talk. Talk is active participation in language, not the study of the techniques of speaking. There is an important difference between a child talking, and a child giving a talk. Ponder on this distinction as you guide teachers to develop classroom talk. Students need to have experiences and to talk about them—to find their potential meaning, which is not always clear at first. "It needs," Dixon suggests, "to be worked over, 'realized' again through language, shared and modified perhaps in the way we apprehend it."[6] By this means we lead students to become spectators, that is, "attentive, immersed onlookers," by which means they share something of the outlook of the artist. Dixon adds,

> When life is felt as immediate and particular, our work in this role is closest to the artist; as it moves towards generality it moves closer to the thinker. Perhaps English holds the middle ground. . . . Pupils with their own experience of the role of spectator have the power, then, to draw from the artist and thinker new insights into life.[7]

In practical terms our task will be to assist teachers in learning how to create situations of talk in the classroom. English teaching as now practiced is so structured that free talk will seem to some teachers to be anarchy. But the spirit of the Dartmouth Seminar makes clear that unless we can foster talk in the classroom many essential values of English will be lost.

### Language

Dixon states further:

> At present we are rather ignorant about three things: first, the ways in which children and young people learn language; second, the conditions and the stages in which they become aware of language they have learnt to use; and third, the effects of such awareness or knowledge on their further learning and operating of language.[8]

In other words, we know so little about how language is learned that we should be most cautious in making assertions, and especially careful of avoiding dogmatism.

The Seminar makes two recommendations about content in language teaching. I summarize the first thus:

a. Latinate grammar does not help students to use language effectively.
b. The new grammars, while interesting, have not yet proved that they help students to use language effectively.
c. Students should be freed from the *disabling conceptions* of "correctness" and "dialect."
d. A positive criterion: lead students outward from their sense of language as an artifact to themselves as organizers of experience in the act of speaking and writing.

The second recommendation is about how knowledge should arise.

    a. Eliminate teaching now what is chiefly useful in the future. Dixon suggests that "ideally, no pupil should ever be given an assignment which does not, at that time in the class, yield him enough fruit in his own terms, so that he can feel it was worth doing." [9]

    b. Linguistic discussions, that is, talk about language, arise from pupils' own questions and observations on the language in actual operation: "How does it work?" is the leading question.

These observations and recommendations have definite implications for what we call grammar. It is very clear that American schools today have more emphasis upon structural analysis than do British schools. I gather from the Seminar that these principles apply to curriculum making and the supervision of teaching in the area of grammar:

    a. We know very little about how much any knowledge of structure aids the use of language.

    b. We can be assured from experience that Latinate (traditional) grammar does not measurably advance the use of language.

    c. The new grammars offer interesting insights into language, but there is as yet no assurance that they actually develop better use of language.

    d. It is folly for teachers to impose heavy bodies of linguistic knowledge on students.

    e. So far as possible, knowledge about language should be the teacher's possession, to create a framework for the students' discoveries about the operation of language.

The whole question of teaching language was summed up by Muller in these words:

> There remains the unanswerable question of just when, what, and how much to teach about the language, but the agreement of the Seminar that English teachers need to have a sound, conscious knowledge of the language means that most teachers need to be retrained and the English curriculum drastically revised.[10]

## Drama

The term drama as used in the Seminar means something very different from what it meant to you and me when we were in high school: to us it meant reading plays as literature, largely studied as texts in silent reading, with perhaps a few scenes acted out. Or else it meant "putting on a play" of dubious literary quality as an extra-curricular activity to entertain the community.

I shall quote some passages from Dixon to clarify the particular significance given to the word "drama" in the Seminar.

> Drama itself arises inevitably from talk: at one moment a pupil is telling the class about stevedores at work; the next he is on his feet, enacting with gesture and movement the poise and grip of the man.[11]

> Drama, then, differs from other talk in three ways: movement and gesture play a larger part in the expression of meaning; a group working together upon an improvisation needs more deliberately and consciously to collaborate . . . ; the narrative framework allows for repetition and provides a unity that enables the action more easily to take on symbolic status.[12]

> Drama, like talk, is learning through interaction.[13]

> From their earliest years, children's simplifications of role and interaction, and the ritual style of their speech, lend themselves to a symbolic presentation of life.[14]

> What is required is an awareness among teachers of English of those moments in a lesson, or in a week's work, when what has been said or read moves naturally out to enactment with movement and gesture. . . . In this inclusiveness drama is central to English work at every level. . . . "Drama" means doing, acting things out rather than working on them in abstract and in private. When possible it is the truest form of learning. . . .[15]

I have quoted rather extensively from the seminar reports because the concept of *drama* presented by the Seminar is almost completely new to American education. It must be apparent from the quotations that "drama" means recreating life itself, freely and voluntarily in the classroom. It means the acting out of experiences, real and imagined, in unstructured impromptu performance combining talk with action. It means the creation of situations that allow the imagination to combine with experience to result in behavior that is free, unself-conscious, and vivid, with genuine emotional involvement.

This approach to life in the classroom is so new and so different from our usual conduct of a class that it will require study and exploration first by us, as supervisors, then specific training of teachers, perhaps a selected few at first, then demonstrations of drama of this kind at teachers' meetings, and finally the adoption of free drama as a technique of language learning at all school levels.

### Writing

Writing becomes realistic when there is experience to relate; the live, active classroom is the matrix from which comes the urge to write. If there is no urge to write, then the classroom and the teacher directing it are inadequate to the need. In American schools we have been bullied by college teachers into assuming that writing means exposition. Exposition means a foundation of facts almost entirely outside oneself, facts of minimum interest, and almost complete lack of personal involvement. To this dull assembly of data we add a formidable battery of techniques: topic sentences, paragraph development, outlining by logical procedures, and organization of relatively meaningless content. This is our usual composition program, and we wonder why students do not write avidly, with genuine interest and profound involvement!

Let us examine some statements of the Dartmouth Seminar on writing. Dixon states:

> To write . . . is to move from the social and shared work [that is, drama] to an opportunity for private and individual work. But the private work takes its meaning from what has gone on before . . . writing-assignments without a background of discussion and shared experience are unlikely to elicit much response from many children and young people.[16]

While talk is personal, writing is largely or completely the medium of the school. The neglect of talk and drama has had disastrous effects on writing because the writer has had nothing to draw upon. Teachers, Dixon says, have grown to look upon writing as the occasion

> "for correcting the propriety and accuracy of the language used." We can view it this way: a sense of the social system of writing has so inhibited and overawed many teachers that they have never given a pupil the feeling that what he writes is his own.[17]

How, then, shall we teach writing to involve the student in a personally vital activity, a thing of his own? Dixon suggests,

> The first factor, then, in helping pupils reach their own decisions in writing . . . is to let exploratory talk precede writing. A second factor is form. It is a common experience that children

and young people enjoy free forms. The deliberate introduction of topic sentence method and stanzas is more likely to prevent their having something to say than assist it. . . . The third factor is perhaps the most insidious. It is the teacher. . . . A teacher of English, one could well say, spends his time in his better hours discovering *through* his pupils.[18]

## Literature as Experience

The reasons for teaching literature are many, and the principal reason underlying the teaching of literature in our schools does not stand out clearly. Most of our curriculums blend in various degrees three basic concepts which might be labelled the Heritage Concept, the Critical Concept, and the Humanistic Concept. To me the emphasis on teaching literature in the Dartmouth reports is essentially humanistic—that is, an intense interrelationship between life itself and the literature reflecting life.

I quote Dixon:

If an interest in literature is to inform and modify our encounter with life itself, the teacher must bring into a vivid relationship life as it is enacted and life as it is represented [in other words, real life and life in literature]. For some of us this means a readiness to go outside the classroom walls, to meet people, observe them, and work with them, so that we and our pupils can draw from their experience and understanding.[19]

Literature has no existence "out there"; the writer's sequences of signs take life from within us, from the personal experiences that we as readers draw on and bring to them. . . . There is no short cut then to each pupil learning to read for himself.[20]

I find in these statements some exceedingly germinal thoughts. First is the intimate and essential relationship between writing and literature. The student writes because he has experiences to relate, to evaluate and to put into the emotional perspective of his life. He is therefore the producer of literature. But he is also the consumer of literature because authors give him experiences to integrate with his own, thus broadening his general reaction to life. Literature, therefore, earns its way into the student's regard by being the extension of what he has already begun to evaluate and appreciate. In this ideal relationship the student reaches out for literature; it is not something external to him to which he must submit. Hence Dixon can conclude,

. . . we look to literature to bring order and control to our world, and perhaps to offer an encounter with difficult areas of experience without exacting from us the full price.[21]

## Organizing for Teaching English

The Dartmouth Seminar aspects do not give specific treatment to the organization of English classes for the maximum benefit of students, but it ought to be apparent that many of the stimulating and challenging ideas from this seminar will not flourish in the traditional English class hours. We are addicted to grade placement and a rigid schedule of class hours of the same length and frequency for all students. Some subjects may possibly be taught superbly in this pattern, but I think no one will challenge me when I say that English is not one of them. Furthermore, rigid scheduling tends to support rigid curriculum patterns, the two together forming a deadlock not easily broken. We know that students vary widely in the performance of skills of communication; we know that they read at widely different rates and maturity levels; we know that some ninth graders write better than many seniors, and some seniors write better than their teachers (composition is the only art in which the paid teachers do not have to demonstrate their own competence). Knowing these and other different factors about students, we still largely herd them into ninth-grade, tenth-grade, eleventh-grade, and twelfth-grade English as though each level was a new subject progressively advanced above the previous one. We know this is not true, and that we are wasting the time of innumerable students who are doing repetitive busy work in skills which they can already perform satisfactorily. By the same token we are condemning to standards of performance beyond them many students who for one reason or another cannot operate at class level. No pious talk about adjusting to individual differences in the classroom can cover up these pedagogical deficiencies.

English is, above all, individual behavior. That concept rises above all others in the Dartmouth reports. It is surprising, therefore, that so few schools and so few departments of English are making any effort to escape the tyranny of grade level progression. We have as evidence many different and effective plans for English organization. A few examples can be found in every state. But why are they so few? These plans include varieties of team teaching, unit group and leader plans, elective unit plans, modular scheduling, ability grouping plans, and the ungraded English program.

We as supervisors and leaders of teachers are failing in a major responsibility if we do not perform these advisory activities:

1. To be adequately informed of all the current plans for

releasing English from the lockstep of rigid grade placement and progression.

2. To seek knowledge of, observe, evaluate, and publicize in our own states these experiments, which are making English a subject based on the competence of performance of its students.

3. To encourage every school and every English department to make a study of a plan for the teaching of English best suited to its own situation, but to attempt to accomplish the goal of permitting each student to perform the skills and activities of English at his own level of competence.

The state supervisor of the language arts is commissioned to lead, to exert pressure for change, to carry the good news of fresh ideas, new materials, and more effective methods. Each of us feels this change and responsibility deeply. But like a battery which gives out energy as it is needed we can become run down. We need constant recharging. I have tried to express in this paper that a valuable source of recharging is the Dartmouth reports.

1. Herbert J. Muller, *The Uses of English* (New York: Holt, Rinehart and Winston, 1967), p. vi. All passages quoted from *The Uses of English* are reprinted by permission of the publisher.

2. John Dixon, *Growth through English* (Huddersfield, England: National Association for the Teaching of English, 1967), p. xi. All passages quoted from *Growth through English* are reprinted by permission of the publisher.

3. Muller, p. 19.

4. Dixon, p. 10.

5. Ibid., p. 13.

6. Ibid., p. 28.

7. Ibid., pp. 29-30.

8. Ibid., p. 76.

9. Ibid., p. 78.

10. Muller, p. 74.

11. Dixon, p. 37.

12. Ibid., p. 37.

13. Ibid., p. 38.

14. Ibid., p. 40.

15. Ibid., pp. 42-43.

16. Ibid., p. 44.

17. Ibid., p. 44.

18. Ibid., pp. 46-47-48.

19. Ibid., p. 54.

20. Ibid., p. 56.

21. Ibid., p. 57.

*If our instruction is to be purposeful then it must, in some way, help students be more effective human beings (that is, more humane) now and in the future. And it must also provide some ways to help students solve problems.*

# Language in School Programs

## by Stanley B. Kegler

"A fable, which Aesop somehow neglected to record, tells of a hen who was making an effort to instruct her chicks about their future sources of food supply while she and they were balanced precariously on a chicken coop which was being carried down a river by a flood. It was a long time since the hen had studied the forests on the bank, and the account she was giving her chicks of forest resources was none too good. So she called to a wise owl on the bank for help. 'You know the woods, O Owl, for you stay in this forest and study it,' said the hen. 'Will you not tell me what to teach my chicks about life in the forest?' But the owl had overheard what the hen had been telling the chicks about the forest as she came along, and he thought it was scientifically inaccurate and superficial. Besides, he was just then very busy completing a monograph on the incidence of beetle

Dr. Stanley B. Kegler
Associate Dean
College of Education
University of Minnesota

13

larvae in acorns. So he pretended he had not heard the hen. The hen, turned back upon herself, proceeded as well as she could to prepare and put into effect an instruction unit on the food resources of oak forests, meanwhile struggling to keep the chicks from falling off the chicken coop. The chicks took the instruction very well, and later the chicken coop stopped at a point far downstream, and the chicks all went ashore—to begin their adult lives in a treeless meadow." [1]

This fable, included by Robert Redfield in *Social Education*, contains a number of lessons or morals, as is true of all classic fables: it describes rather well the present state of teacher preparation programs; it goes to the current question of the "relevance" of what we study in our schools and how we study it; and most importantly in this context, it describes the gap which characterizes the relationship between language scholars and teachers in our schools.

We face many of the same problems in teaching English that the little hen did in teaching her chicks about the food resources of the forests, and we run the same risks that our instruction will be as meaningless and as useless as the hen's was. If our instruction is to be purposeful then it must, in some way, help students be more effective human beings (that is, more humane) now and in the future. And it must also provide some ways to help students solve problems.

As we look to the question of what should be incorporated in the language instruction in our schools, I feel that several cautions are in order. For our purposes here, I have chosen to differentiate between language study and linguistics. The two are often equated. I have seen school programs that are described in glowing terms, but often the program is confined solely to the study of one kind of grammar. Language study to me is broad and humane; it is far more inclusive than the study of structures and relationships, which is frequently as far as "linguistic" study goes. Language study involves not only the nature of language, how the language is structured, but also how language is learned and used in a society which prides itself on the use of the word.

It is difficult, of course, to speak of language study without asking the perennial question bugging English teachers: "Will it help students be better readers, writers, and speakers?" Posing a question such as this, of course, assumes that this is one of the important jobs of the school program. I should like to pose that task more broadly by suggesting that the major task facing all of us is helping young people learn how to solve as yet unknown problems in unknown ways. Learning how to think and determining what is worth thinking about is the job of our schools.

As we determine the content and processes of school programs, we must also note how those programs are—or can be—organized. Perhaps at no time in our history has greater discussion been generated regarding the nature and boundaries of the subject. The shape of English, of course, has been rather well defined historically. The answer which we are given today —that the shape of our curriculum is a rather vaguely defined "blob" including language, literature, and composition—is not a new answer. That definition of English has a striking affinity to the definition given the subject by the chairman of the English Conference of the Committee of Ten of the NEA in 1892, when the answer was only slightly transposed to literature, language, and composition.

Teachers of the language arts have long been dissatisfied with a curriculum which appeared to have an inherent tendency toward fragmentation. We have tried to revise and develop a coherent pattern for the teaching of English for 75 years; we have tried to find an integrating point out from which teachers could move in the subject they teach. The ill-defined tripod of language, literature, and composition is relatively meaningless because it does not provide an integrating focus for curriculum development. It lays out the boundaries, but it does not identify a center. Within the perimeter, as all of us know, there is a good deal of wandering about. A vague and broad definition of our subject will not do. We cannot simply respond by saying that English is an accident or that it is a tripod of two knowledges and one skill or that it is a hodgepodge and there is nothing that we can do about it. Nor can we, as John Dixon suggests, define a process through ". . . a description of the activities we engage in through language."[2] What is this thing called "process" about which we hear and read a good deal lately? Is it, for example, an individual process by which thought takes place? Is it the interaction process of a group as it arrives at consensus or collective action? Is it a set of protocols or activities engaged in by individuals or groups? We simply do not have readily available guidance which will help us sort out what is reasonable and useful in the English classroom. What *is* needed, as H. A. Gleason has observed, is an integrating center around which an English curriculum can be built.[3]

This cultural hangup goes back to the period before the turn of the century when the apostles of the genteel tradition sat in the chairs of English in our major colleges. The temper of what goes on in our college classes is still influenced by the genteel tradition. Is it any wonder that teachers of English, especially in our senior high schools, often feel isolated and alienated—especially from the disadvantaged? Is it possible that the culture we are trying so hard to preserve and pass on is irrelevant, or even dead? Is it possible that the major stream of the culture has been diverted, and, as the guardians of that culture, we are left high and dry?

Another problem which English teachers have faced and still face relates to the doctrine of utility, to which I referred earlier. As in almost no other subject of the curriculum, teachers of the language arts always seem to be wanting an answer to the questions, "Will it work?" "Is it practical?" "Will it help my students become more effective readers, writers, speakers, listeners, or whatever?" In no other subject do we concern ourselves so centrally with "usefulness."

Sometimes the language arts teacher is able to effect a kind of connubial bliss between culture and utility in dealing with problems of usage and correctness in writing. Here the teacher can clearly develop cultural values (by emphasizing a "proper" standard of usage), while at the same time showing that ability to speak well and write well (which means "correctly") will command more dollars and cents in the secretarial market. This is best typified by the way in which teachers go about the job of "correcting" papers. We know almost nothing about the process of writing; we deal with it as a product. That is, we know next to nothing about what goes on inside a kid's head between the time he puts his pencil to paper and the time he picks it back up. Yet it is during this interval that the process of composition is going on. The product, if one reflects on the practices of most teachers, is one which *obviously* requires "correction" even before we have examined the papers to know if anything is wrong. We assume what Roger Shuy has called the "Al Capone Syndrome"—the eradication of errors at any cost. Clearly our practice reveals that we think we can modify language behavior; yet, as English teachers, how much do we know about verbal behavior, language acquisitions, language modification? As a result of these hangups and the inadequate answers given to the question about what English is, we have not derived that integrating center around which the new curriculum in language arts can be built and which H. A. Gleason hoped for.

In addition, we face today a new kind of problem which teachers even twenty years ago did not have to face. This problem is a result of inputs from new sources of information which confront the language teacher who honestly believes that a teacher of English is a teacher of language nature and functions. Some time ago I asked one of my students to list the topics included in one month's issues of three different periodicals which deal with the teaching of English. When limited to the area of language, the topics included were: psycholinguistics, linguistic science, transformational grammar, generative grammar, computational grammar, Cartesian linguistics, tagmemics, proxemics, kinesics, structural grammar, stratificational grammar, lexicostatistics, historical linguistics, lexicography, sociolinguistics, language culture studies, anthropology, rhetorical studies, contemporary logic, symbolic logic, communication and discourse theory, and semantics.

This list clearly demonstrates new sources of information not commonly included in teacher preparation programs. It also suggests that English teachers are by definition teachers of language, and they had better be informed of how language is acquired, developed, and manipulated. We are teachers of language, and one of our major jobs is to help students learn to modify their own language behavior by more facile language manipulations. There are other inputs, too, from learning theory, especially through the evolution of what might be called the "additive concept" rather than the "replacement concept" as we work on language development of young people. It is becoming increasingly clear that the latter approach is ineffective and that it must be replaced by the former.

I think it is reasonable at this point in our history to allege that the guiding philosophy in language study in the schools of tomorrow will be focused around the integrating center of language study. Regardless of the specific emphasis that individuals would place on the study of language, thoughtful students of curriculum in English tend to agree that the core of our discipline is language. This *core* is mentioned in a variety of articles, speeches, and books far too frequently to document here. I think that the simplest statement is that which the Commission on English of the College Entrance Examination Board made in 1965. That Commission stated bluntly in the introduction to *Freedom and Discipline in English* that its statements about the subject of English were based ". . . on the unstartling assumption that the core of our discipline is language." [4]

Why am I so convinced that a language-based curriculum will form the integrating center for the language arts curriculum? The philosophical foundation for this belief is found in a statement I helped prepare for the Language Arts Department of University High School at the University of Minnesota some ten years ago. Let me quote from that statement:

> We believe that the proper concern of the English curriculum is the study of man himself and that the most vital information about man can be found through the study of the language he uses. We believe that the study of language, broadly conceived, will reveal how man views himself, by what

and for what man lives, and how man orders his existence. We believe that the most clearly observable feature of humanity is man's ability to manipulate verbal symbols in a complex way. As the Danish linguist Hjelmelev puts it, "it is in language that we find the distinctive mark of personality, for good or ill, the distinctive mark of home and of nation, mankind's patent of nobility." We believe that understanding the operations and the nature of language is of central importance in an open society, which must, by the nature of its political and social structures, make decisions affecting group and individual actions.

Our goal is the education of linguistically sensitive persons. By this we mean persons aware of influencing and being influenced through language, conscious of the multiple ways in which language operates, appreciative of the artistic use of language, as in literature, and informed about the nature of the language they use. As speakers and writers, our students should be aware of their responsibilities to make and support assertions using appropriate language and patterns of thought. As listeners and readers, our students should be aware of their responsibilities to evaluate the assertions of others. Our students should be conscious of the variety of human functions performed through language. Our students should be appreciative of the artistic use of language in varieties of literature, the uses of language which offer special insight into human experience. Our students should be informed about the symbolic quality and structural characteristics of the language they use.

A common element in all of our concerns is language, its uses and its nature. This concern is proper, we believe, because we live, using the figure of Neils Bohr, the great Danish nuclear physicist, "suspended in language." [5]

The conviction that this kind of philosophy emphasizes allows for the development of a curriculum that looks to the future as well as the present and the past. It allows for a development of the notion that language is thought and thought is language. (Please note that I did not say that language provides the tools for thought; I said that language *is* thought and thought *is* language.) If you accept this point of view then we had better worry about the business of teaching language and focus our instruction on that problem.

On purely pragmatic grounds I am also convinced that what is needed is a language-based curriculum. The present status of the curriculum in English can be characterized as disjointed, fragmented, and disordered. Little attention is given to the nature, structure and functions of the language itself. Instruction in the history of the language, in the problems of meaning, reference and proof, in media influences, in the forms of discourse, and in the relationships between language and culture, is incomplete and unsystematic. The relationships between instruction about language as provided in English classes, and that provided in speech, journalism and foreign languages is not clear, even though such courses presumably give some instruction about language.

The most consistent aspect of instruction about language in the high school curriculum is that of grammar. This instruction is still generally limited (in the majority of our schools) to prescriptive statements about usage which are derived from the Graeco-Latinate grammar of the eighteenth century, with little awareness of the great body of English grammar based upon nineteenth century philology, to say nothing of the impressive findings in English linguistics during the past generation. Instruction in prescriptive grammar rests upon the assumptions that improvement in usage will result or that mental discipline will accrue. Substantial research has disproved both assumptions. A third assumption has been honored neither in recognition nor in applications, namely, that the kind of grammar which provides realistic information about the nature and structure of English might well be studied in and for itself, as a humanistic pursuit. In short, the one aspect of language instruction receiving some attention, grammar, is not taught systematically, or with a defensible rationale, or in terms of reputable contemporary knowledge about language.

The bulk of instruction in grammar is dependent on the so-called "series" texts in composition and grammar. Many are woefully inadequate; not infrequently the information given refers not to the structure of English, but to that of Latin. Frequently the textbook writers themselves reveal a rather profound linguistic and psychological confusion by mixing precepts about spoken and written discourse. Probably the chief deficiency lies in the repetitive nature of the materials themselves. The tendency is to start each text in the same place—the *ab ovo* approach—(usually with a discussion of the parts of speech) and end a little beyond the material covered in the previous year's text. There are serious omissions—it is still a rare text, for example, that takes real account of the fact that one of the prime features of the structure of the English language is word order and that the relationships among words in syntactic strings is not at all the same as the words studied individually.

This rather bleak appraisal is not to suggest that no work is being done to try to find an integrating core out of which English teachers can find a rationale for their work. Several large and many small institutions, school systems, and agencies have undertaken special programs to more clearly identify the goals of English instruction. The Project English Centers have provided an opportunity for teachers in the field to examine curriculum materials—not all of them oriented toward language study—from which to choose. As I indicated earlier, I am hopeful that these centers have provided English teachers with enough differing kinds of materials so that they can answer for themselves the questions about what English is. I am persuaded that the core of that study is language, but I am equally persuaded that you need not necessarily agree with me but should find your own answer.

You might wish, for example, to consider replacing the content-centered approach to literature, which the Basic Issues Conference of 1958 so heavily stressed, with an emphasis on experience and involvement, one of the major changes of focus resulting from the Dartmouth Seminar of 1966. I would suggest that the dichotomy between a content-centered approach and an emphasis upon experience and involvement is irrelevant and that an emphasis on experience and involvement *can* be effected simultaneously with studies of the nature and uses of language. The content does, in major ways, determine method. For language, either individually or socially, as a reflection of individual experience or experience of the race, must in its very essence, be a matter of experience and involvement.

Previously I indicated that teachers must be concerned with what may be to many the unanswerable question—how to teach in order to help students solve unknown problems in unknown ways. I also posed the question of what the program in English should be.

Let me answer the latter question first. The English curriculum of tomorrow will bear little resemblance in either spirit or detail to the present, largely because of what I perceive as an emerging focus on language study—which is now still largely ignored. Language study itself will take on new dimensions so that it takes into account the variety of information about language which should inform curriculum development and the teaching of the language arts. It will be considerably broader than grammar, whatever the brand of grammar, which I believe will be pluralistic, and will focus on the uses of language as well as the nature of language. I am convinced that it will deal with how we use language and how language is used to affect us and our decisions. It will deal with how language is acquired and how language is developed. It will deal with the relationships between things and the words that are used to describe and classify and categorize these things—man's view of his world. It will deal with grammar and grammatical questions, not to help students become better writers or speakers, but to help them understand what this uniquely human attribute is all about and, of course, to help them synthesize experience in order to come to terms with reality. It will deal with the problems of understanding metaphor in language. It will deal with sets of rhetorical principles to help students understand what the process of composing—oral and written—is all about.

Now let me try to suggest what I think the answer is to the unknown problems which must be solved in unknown ways and how language arts teachers working with students now can make an impact on those unknown problems a generation from now. It is impossible at this juncture to predict what those unknown problems will be. It also seems clear to me that we must structure our work so that we will prepare students to deal with those problems as yet unknown and to work toward solving those problems with tools as yet undeveloped or unrefined. The one thing which seems certain is that the manipulation of verbal symbols—because it is part and parcel of the thought processes— will play an important role in the solution of human problems. That is, any problems which are likely to be faced will be "suspended in language." The solution of these problems will depend on students' abilities to manipulate language—to manipulate thought processes, or, if you will, to synthesize experience on the grid of language. The major goal of a language focus is not, as is often alleged, the achieving of mastery of cultivated usage, writing, and speaking. Its goal is to assure neither the development of mental discipline nor facility in learning another language. It is, rather, to achieve the commendable humanistic end of understanding man's most significant achievement—the development of an ability to manipulate verbal symbols so that the student can communicate, solve problems, carry on daily activities, pass on the heritage, and think about his future.

If we believe that learning is the process of opening doors, then I think we must keep in mind that those doors open only from the inside. The keeper of the keys is the learner himself and no amount of prying or shoving will open the doors unless the learner permits. Only the learner can give us access, but when he does, I hope we will enter with the understanding that the real art of teaching is facilitating, not inhibiting, and that one of the really important results of language sensitivity and understanding is the achievement of facility in dealing with problems. A body of knowledge is, after all, only a frame of reference helpful in the solution of problems. That body of knowledge is useful only if the children we teach are able to use the referent process in problem solving situations. Mastery of this comes, of course, with the subtle, sensitive understanding of what language is and what it can do. Some students will achieve it *without* us or *despite* us. I would like to believe that all students will achieve it *because* of us.

1. Robert Redfield, "Research in the Social Studies: Its Significance for General Education," *Social Education*, 5 (December 1941), p. 568. Reprinted by permission of the National Council for the Social Studies.

2. John Dixon, *Growth through English* (London: National Association for the Teaching of English, 1967), p. 7.

3. H. A. Gleason, "What is English?" *CCCC* (October 1962), pp. 1-10.

4. Commission on English, *Freedom and Discipline in English* (New York: College Entrance Examination Board, 1965), p. 2.

5. Stanley B. Kegler and Rodger Kemp, *A Philosophy for the Language Arts Program* (University High School, University of Minnesota, 1961). Mimeo.

*If we are going to make poetry available to our pupils, and I think we ought, then we should do so as auspiciously as possible, especially to establish a community of interest, a community of attentiveness and responsiveness. Let them discover a new world in the familiar world, their community that includes not only the poets but also the kids, painters, photographers, and artists of various kinds, and the folk traditions. We should think as far as possible, not only about the kinds of books that we get the kids, but beyond the books.*

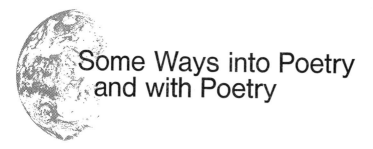

# Some Ways into Poetry and with Poetry

## by Geoffrey Summerfield

When we consider some ways into poetry and with poetry, the question that strikes men is quite simply, what could conceivably be more marginal to our age, to the dominant concerns of our society, than the reading of poetry? Consult lists of best sellers for the last twenty or thirty or forty years and where are the poets? They are conspicuous by their absence. How often do poets appear on television during prime time? I suppose one answer is that they appear when, like Robert Frost, they have been taken up by the establishment. Too often

**Professor Geoffrey Summerfield**
Lecturer in Education and English
Langwith College
University of York, Heslington

23

students show the deepest antipathy and a sense of tedium for poetry. On such evidence poetry seems to be arid, unproductive, empty, and washed up. It has an uninteresting past, a questionable present, and no future at all.

But turn the coin over and be prepared to be blinded by the glare. First of all, ask any responsible European man of letters where he locates the most interesting and productive areas of contemporary writing and the consensus of answers will include, near the top of the list, American poetry of the past fifteen years —a poetry which is characterized by abundance, diversity, seriousness, experimentalism, intelligence, passion, and technical competence of a very high order. Again, look at the publications of the underground press syndicate and at the long playing records of progressive rock and soul and of the innumerable progeny of the Beatles and what do you find? You find a proliferation of modes, representing experiences which are undeniably nearer to poetry than to anything else.

Now what we have is a paradox which is rich in ironic suggestiveness, a situation that in its bafflements and its range of ironies would have been worthy of Henry James.

Take this stance of concern, of bafflement, of puzzlement, and of sheer involvement. I am partisan, I think the word matters. I want to place the plea for ways with poetry at various times and in various places both private and public, dramatic and even theatrical, that come close at times to a melting pot of all the arts that are often speculative, sometimes improper, controversial, dangerous, student-centered, prodigal, attentive to what makes the kids tick. I plead for ways that are both passive and active and that are, above all, free of academicism. But now for some personal notes, a few hints of what seems to me to be one way toward a diagnosis of the present situation.

Briefly I think we have gone seriously wrong with poetry, even with literature generally, and I am using poetry, in fact, as a very special intensive location for literature in general. To put the matter crudely, we have made the mistake of doing not "our thing," not "their thing," but somebody else's "thing." And that somebody else is in some way our alter ego. That person, the persona, exercises a deep and often unexamined influence on our own assumptions and our own practices. Often it is the university professor, a person from our own past, more or less recent, for whom we have intellectual respect and whose good opinion we have at some stage in our development needed. The influence of the university professor has made itself felt in two main ways: in our choice of repertoire and in *modus operandi*, our ways of relating the teacher, the taught, and the text. As far as the repertoire is concerned, we have adopted what a consensus of respected opinion would recognize as in some sense the heritage. As far as the *modus operandi* is concerned, there are again, I think, interesting similarities and significant differences. What the American teacher does with the poem in the classroom is what the British teacher also tends to do. That is, he does what his elders and betters at the university did. The dominant orthodoxy in Britain, therefore, is to involve the kids in some gross parody of the activities of the literary critic, of the literary scholar, or of the literary historian. In America, the bias, I would imagine, would probably move in the direction of an analysis of poetry that demonstrates the way in which a poem exemplifies essential characteristics of the genre to which the poem is said to belong. But both systems share this distinctive quality. Both rest on the assumption that before the lesson starts, the teacher knows the answers to the questions that he intends to pose about the poem. In both cases, the poem is the datum which is to be submitted to an analysis. In both instances, the prime activity is analysis of something that is there in the classroom, in the word on the page. In both instances, the reasons why that particular poem is there in the classroom have very little, if anything, to do with who the kids are or what the time is. And the time is later than we think. At its worst, the poem is there because the poem is bound to occur on the next page of the English series used in the school. The kinds of lunacies that these activities give rise to can be encaptured, I think, very briefly, for my present purposes.

In England a failure of response on the part of the pupil is construed as a failure on the part of the pupil or the student, not as a failure on the part of the teacher, *not* as a symptom of an inappropriate choice of material by the teacher.

In America, to choose at random, one meets such assertions as the following: "Literature is an art field having its own stylistic devices and its own structures or forms. If students are to understand what a literary work has to say, they must learn the most important of the conventions." The stress in that particular formulation falls clearly on the existence of an *a priori* body of knowledge which the teacher is to mediate. The argument rests, it seems to me, on the confusion about the nature of understanding. What the writer seems to have intended is not, in fact, understanding, but rather the ability of the student to talk about literature in the way in which the teacher expects the student to be able to talk about literature, which is not necessarily understanding. The argument is this: in specific terms the child of ten, for example, will not understand what *Beowulf* has to say unless he learns the most important of conventions operating in the composition of an early English epic poem. Now such an argument rests on a pedantic, esoteric, falsely academic notion about understanding.

This seems to derive from the assumption that a school's task is to rehearse such activities as these to be performed again at a college or university with much more finesse, style, precision, and completeness. If Matthew Arnold's conception of the education of adolescents was to see it as a preparation for life, the present orthodoxy seems to me to see it as a preparation for the next stage of education or instruction and all in the sacrosanct, the spiral curriculum.

Let's consider *Beowulf*, since the poem interests me at the moment. My most recent experience with a poem in the classroom in England was, to put it mildly, excruciating. A postgraduate student teacher, just fresh from finals, unloaded on a class of twelve-year-old girls all her recently acquired Anglo-Saxon scholarship, her philology, her comparative linguistics, her socio-anthropological background. She was just starting to teach, she was just fresh from the university lecture room, so I made allowances. In her wealth of pedantry, of rhetorical analysis, of stylistics, in her wealth of history and of geography, the students lost the pity and the terror, the gut-twisting horror, the gleams of light in the dark, fearsome world, in short, the simultaneous external reality, and internal, felt truth of the poem. Some of these twelve-year-old kids knew what to do with *Beowulf*. During the apparently interminable lecture, some of them passed notes, others scratched hearts and graphics on their desks. Some wrote love letters and stuffy poems. One or two were trying to read the poem, their lips moving, stumbling through the dark wood of words.

Now, the job of the secondary school teacher in this sort of situation seems to be simpler yet more complex than that of the university teacher. It is best to allow something to happen, to allow the student to experience the poem by first handling it in the most congenial way possible. And since the poem in this particular case was an oral poem, part of an oral tradition, it should obviously be taken by the ear, rather than by the eye. And since it is a long, but intense poem, it needs to be taken in parts, the first parts taken as close together as possible in time.

Reading aloud is a taxing activity and one that calls for skill of a high order: performing skills, interpretative skills, dramatic skills. The teacher must think twice before tackling it and, having chosen it, must prepare the performance of the poem very thoroughly, editing, making judicious cuts, perhaps reinforcing the work with music and even blacking out the room and having just one spot of light on the face of the speaker.

Rather an extraordinary effort, you may cry, but an ideal opportunity for collaboration between two or three teachers taking classes of comparable levels to share the load, to set up a reciprocal system of give and take. The kind of performance that I envision with *Beowulf*, with kids, would be spectacular in a sense.

Relate this further to the contemporary cult of the psychedelic, then take a look at the physical setting of most English lessons in most schools today: the environmental, the sensory, the aesthetic barrenness of many of our high school English rooms. They are sterile, perfunctory, institutionalized bleakness. For many of our students nothing happens in those uninviting and unexciting square rooms. I would like, therefore, to propose the obliteration of our inherited and cherished barriers between official and unofficial culture and specifically to propose that we think of the lessons that we show our students in terms of active stratagem. Let us consider the repertoire of our culture for a moment.

Start with Sidney, who is twelve and black and comes from the poor side of Lincoln, Nebraska. We don't have a ghetto in Lincoln, we just have a poorer side. His home is in an area of the city that isn't mentioned in the official Chamber of Commerce brochure. It is characterized by the co-existence of poor, rickety furniture and a large-screen television set. His record in school has been one of indifference and he is now in sixth grade. He hadn't shown any fondness for books. The other day he was rather tired. He explained that he and his sister had sat up until two o'clock in the morning and had read together as far as page 120 of the first book that he had ever taken, of his own volition, home from school. The book was *Selected Poems* written by Langston Hughes. Now, poetry matters to him and I believe it matters profoundly. It is not because we can demonstrate our audition on it. It is not because it exemplifies genre theory, it is not because we use rhetorical devices that we can put clever names to. It has to do with the capacity to make recognizable and vivid, urgent and hilarious, memorable and vivifying, representations of our world and of ourselves. It is not decorative, and it is not prettifying; it is not an electric motor to be taken apart, and it is not a reassurance, at least not in the sort of bourgeoisie sense of providing a cancellation of our prejudices. But above all, I think it is not a respectable, respected canon for heritage which we can hand down like colonists or missionaries in order to civilize lesser mortals. But at this moment in time, it may well be that the most important poetry is a poetry of distinctiveness, the poetry in which the black student can recognize both his Negro ancestry and his Americanism, in which the urban student can recognize his distinctive urbanism, in which the American Indian can more surely know and reclaim his own distinctiveness. It should be the poetry through which each of us can know and be and do with a clearer and sharper integrity, his own "thing."

In the recent past, I am convinced that the heritage has been used unwittingly as an assault on identity, as a means of displacing the self and its own distinctiveness with something superior, eclectic, confused, and officially sanctioned. And nowhere does this do more harm than with adolescents. We who are here managed somehow to survive. We learned to play the game and to perform the tricks that our teachers required of us. We learned to make sounds about Wordsworth or about Pope or about Spenser that were more or less acceptable. We performed the tricks. We didn't switch off, because we wanted the prizes that went to those who appeared to stay switched on. But I think we were a peculiar minority. The majority just didn't want to know. And they didn't want to know, it seems to me, because the poets who were thrust under their noses simply didn't speak to them. And they didn't want to know because the activities that they were made to engage in—scrutiny of rhyme scheme, internal structure of sonic form were piddling, and trivial, and mindless. Or if you like, they were exercises of the mind but not activities that exercised the real self, the whole self.

Well, what have I got to offer? I don't want to sell poetry as such. I don't think poetry in that sense matters. What I would like to do is to set up a bit of creative climate of opinion in which kids will turn to a poem with as much unaffected interest as they turn to a game, to an amusement arcade, to a joke, a piece of gossip, a conversation, an argument, tomorrow's paper, a pop song, or a magazine. In other words, I want to get to the turn to the poetry without affectation in the private domain and in the world which is not dominated by the teacher. I want them, like Sidney, to be able to sit up until two o'clock in the morning, reading about somebody who speaks about the world that they themselves know, who helps them to identify themselves. And I think that it is possible only when we have made available to the kids a plenitude of paperbacks, when we've learned to spend our money, such as it is, on real books, when we learn to take our own books, our own private possessions, into the classroom and just leave them around for the kids to swipe, to take home. We must learn to make books available to the kids by not having any designs on them, by not trying to teach them anything in the public domain, the domain of the classroom. I want a situation in which the teacher or the student will say, "Hey, listen to this! I just read this. What do you think about it?" I call for a situation in which this representation of life will coexist with those other more informal representations of life we call conversation, chat, anecdotage, and exchange. What I don't want to do is to put poetry in a cage called a poetry lesson as if it existed only inside a bizarre zoo containing odd and eccentric and exotic communications, where the poems begin and end within the bars of that cage, having no life, no activity outside it.

Take another sort of situation. In teaching poetry start with the kinds of lives of students with their own sense of life. Use the poem as adjunct, as reflection, as comment, as spotlight, as response to what the kids themselves have to bring to us. Say in effect that this poem exists in the same real world as the things that you have to say about your pigeons, or your new bicycle, or your new girl friend. It is the same world as the impulse that moves you to laugh, to shout, to write graffiti, or to hasten to a friend to share a secret or a discovery. As the response of the poem takes form, it becomes what happened to *me*. This is the essential test to anything more sophisticated or more complex.

I want now to stress the field of active performance. Let us lean to becoming autonomous rather than to operating by rules laid down for us by others. Adequate repertoires of poetry will include plenty of poetry for performance (and by performance I don't mean material for elocution, I don't mean material which is to be exhibited to the proud parents on parents' evening. I don't mean something that merely uses the poem as a starting point and then moves on to something else, a very dramatic improvisation or the painting of a picture). I mean, rather, performance that works into the words of the poem, performance, that is, that represents any interpretation of the poem. That involves again a collaborative act of interpretations in performance, the performance that is by its very nature an interpretation. I think that is the simplest, least-elaborated level. What I have in mind is simply reading a poem aloud, a reading aloud that is as good as we can make it and not merely thrown off or thrown away. But I think also that performance of poetry moves toward the multi-dimensional possibilities of the theater. It moves toward the resources of music, of sound, of noise, and of silence. It involves, at every stage, acts of improvisation which are a form of thinking aloud. Thinking aloud is peculiarly crucial at every stage in our development.

Let me enter one little parenthesis here. If you ask me for the most depressing single characteristic of first-year graduates reading English at the University of York, it is their inability or their unwillingness to think about it, to extemporate, to make rough sketches, to play with and entertain ideas in states of bliss rather than order or finish. It is an unwillingness to expose their confusion and tentativeness and their uncertainty. They want to deliver a poem but it must be final, it must be well-shaped, it must be of the order of a well-made essay. Now with this kind of unwillingness, this kind of inability, this kind of nervousness about the tentativeness, the securitiveness, the indirection becomes a very sad reflection of what has happened to them in their education. In our performance of the poetry we think aloud, we swap ideas, responses, impressions. We try to articulate at the very fringe of our articulacy and we see whatever is at hand that will reinforce reading. We learn that our environment needs help, and we've got to learn to resist our nervousness, to fight our nervousness about crossing frontiers. One of the unfortunate results of our education, especially in Britain, is that we come out of our universities as English specialists, and God help us if we dare to allow anything else to enter into our English lesson whether it is music or the visual arts or whatever. Look at the visual illiteracy of most books produced by teachers of English. We have to resist our nervousness about crossing frontiers, because frontiers aren't in the nature of things. They are merely erected by the traditions of our education.

The active remaking of another person's poem is often as satisfying as the act of making our own. In our own moods and our own to's and fro's, it is often more satisfying. And when I say poetry, what I really mean is the intensity and the relative brevity of the poem and its occasional proximity to other rhythmic forms such as the march, the round, the dance. There are characteristics there which are virtues for us when our lessons are bounded by the clock or the bell, when we have only forty-five minutes in which to operate. There is also a peculiar virtue in the verbal density of poetry, its specific gravity. I think that a distinct virtue for a lot of kids is the kind of verbal intoxication they get.

If we are going to make poetry available to our pupils, and I think we ought, then we should do so as auspiciously as possible, especially to establish a community of interest, a community of attentiveness and responsiveness. Let them discover a new world in the familiar world, their community that includes not only the poets but also the kids, painters, photographers, and artists of various kinds, and the folk traditions. We should think as far as possible, not only about the kinds of books that we get the kids, but beyond the books.

# Traditional vs. Innovative Approaches

## Part Two

*If grammar is conceived of as the attempt to explain how we are able to form sentences—novel sentences, almost effortlessly— how infants acquire language, how one interprets or is able to understand sentences, then it seems to me that the notion of grammar has been vastly expanded. It would include even the study of poetry.*

# Syntax and Meaning

# by Frank J. Zidonis

One can grasp the changing directions of a field of study by noting the new expressions that appear first in scholarly journals, are soon adopted in broader publications, and subsequently recur frequently in the professional literature. This procedure can illuminate the change taking place in the study of language. Among the crucial terms that have followed this route we find the following:

Kernel Sentence and Transform
Deep Structure and Surface Structure
Performance and Competence
Theory of Syntax
Language Acquisition

Dr. Frank J. Zidonis
Associate Professor of English Education
Ohio State University

34

Now a study that is connected with all of the terms mentioned above is necessarily a far-ranging one. Consequently, if we label this study *grammatical study*, we must be ready to define *grammar* so that it is not narrowly conceived. And syntax, I might add, is grammar without the phonology.

Grammar, as the transformationalist understands it, is a system of rules that corresponds to the competence of the native speaker. It is a theory that tries to show how sound and meaning are interrelated, how sentences are formed and understood. Investigating the structure of a theory that deals with sentence formation can increase understanding of language acquisition and language development. The empirical investigation of language acquisition and language development in turn can lead to increased understanding of the logical structure of the theory. How language is learned is a puzzling, controversial topic for the psychologist. And although virtually every child acquires a language, what he does in learning it is nevertheless a remarkable accomplishment. As Noam Chomsky points out in his review of Skinner's book, *Verbal Behavior:*

> It is not easy to accept the view that a child is capable of constructing an extremely complex mechanism for generating a set of sentences, some of which he has heard, or that an adult can instantaneously determine whether (and if so, how) a particular item is generated by this mechanism, which has many of the properties of an abstract deductive theory. Yet this appears to be a fair description of the performance of the speaker, listener, and learner. If this is correct, we can predict that a direct attempt to account for the actual behavior of speaker, listener, and learner, not based on a prior understanding of the structure of grammars, will achieve very limited success. The grammar must be regarded as a component in the behavior of the speaker and listener which can only be inferred . . . from the resulting physical acts. The fact that all normal children acquire essentially comparable grammars of great complexity with remarkable rapidity suggests that human beings are somehow specially designed to do this, with data-handling, or "hypothesis-formulating" ability of unknown character and complexity.[1]

Children have more competence in language than the linguist is yet able to describe; that is, they know more grammar than has been codified. This competence is simply the knowledge they possess about their language which enables them to create and to understand sentences, many of which are completely new for them. It is the goal of the linguist to write a grammar that reveals the nature of this knowledge.

How does he go about the task of writing such a grammar? He must abstract an idealized theory of this often unconscious knowledge from the actual performance of the native speaker. It must be abstracted inasmuch as performance is often distorted by various distractions and memory limitations. We all know how to add and subtract, of course, and yet most of us have probably had difficulty reconciling our checking accounts with the bank's statement.

The next question to raise is this: What does the grammar attempt to do? What does each of the three competing systems of grammatical accounts do with the language? Notice that my discussion takes up traditional, structural, and transformational grammar, omitting both the stratificational and the tagmemic. I'm sure all of us had the experience of the high school student, especially, who comes out of the Latin class and confides to his English teacher, "You know, I really didn't understand English grammar until I had a year of Latin." And for some reason I think teachers always reacted wrongly to this experience; they justified the teaching of Latin instead of questioning the way the English language was being represented. What kind of English are we studying, a student might probably wonder, if it takes a knowledge of Latin grammar to make some of the points of the English grammar come through? The structural grammarian sought to change this paradox.

Probably the structuralist who most influenced the classroom teacher of English is Charles Fries, with his *American English Grammar* and *Structure of English*. *Structure of English* and the Paul Roberts' popular text heavily indebted to it, *Patterns of English*, are most responsible for introducing teachers to the structural system.[2] In usage matters, a great deal of *American English Grammar*, I think, is as relevant today as it was revolutionary in 1940.[3] The structuralists begin their study of language by attending to the signalling system that the sounds of the language reveal. This very starting point, this assumption about the nature of language, has become controversial. The transformationalists tend to say that language is primary, a quite different position from the structuralist's view that language is primarily speech. Fries perhaps did the most of any of the structural grammarians in bringing these phonological techniques to the attention of the classroom teacher of English, especially on the secondary level. His impact on secondary English departments was considerably strengthened by the federally financed Summer Institute Programs, for the Fries text was quite often adopted for the participants. The structuralist produces inventory of elements. He does a great deal of classification and his position would be that the final total of all of the classifications, all of the inventories taken together, becomes a grammar of the language. He always needs a corpus, which should be very carefully defined. In *Structure of English,* for example, Fries used fifty hours of telephone conversations, recorded from calls made to a governmental bureau.[4] The relatively clean classifications he finally came up with stand as a remarkable achievement, especially when one considers the number of throat clearings, repetitions, and unmeaningful utterances that occurred in the corpus of fifty hours. But the technology of the structuralist, the careful control he had over his procedures, was excellent.

There are criteria here for establishing form classes that work for the teacher and work equally well for the student. For example, as most of you know, the Friesian term, Form Class 1 Word, would be one that fits a particular frame of language. Paul Roberts came along later and gave these form classes a more traditional name, though warning that the usual traditional definition did not accompany the traditional label. This kind of systemic formality proves easier to comprehend and apply in fact than the circularity that the traditional or pseudo-traditional definitions get students involved in.

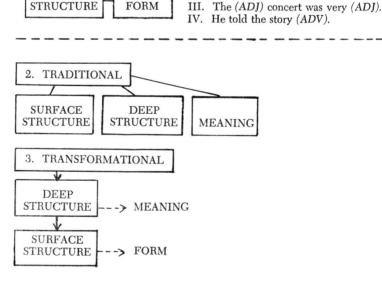

Figure 1

1. STRUCTURAL

SURFACE STRUCTURE — FORM

"Substitution in FRAMES"

I. The *(N)* was good.
II. He *(V)* his tax.
III. The *(ADJ)* concert was very *(ADJ).*
IV. He told the story *(ADV).*

2. TRADITIONAL

SURFACE STRUCTURE | DEEP STRUCTURE | MEANING

3. TRANSFORMATIONAL

DEEP STRUCTURE - -> MEANING

SURFACE STRUCTURE - -> FORM

I've separated two boxes here under "structural." But I point out here that the structuralist is concerned with the surface structure, that is, the actual sound of the utterance. The form of the utterance is largely what he uses in making the classification. His rigorous methodology prevents him from resorting to ellipsis in order to account for any kind of expression. The traditionalist and the transformationalist, on the other hand, would have no compunction against using what is not there to explain what is there. It would not be entirely true to say that the structuralist avoids meaning entirely. One can go back to Leonard Bloomfield to read that semantics has a necessary role in analyzing language; Charles Fries, of course, has much to say here about lexical meaning versus structural meaning. In practice, reliance on meaning is carefully controlled and, to a large extent, is really ignored in this classification scheme. Instead, reliance is placed chiefly on formal considerations, making it more likely for students to arrive at the same classifications as their teachers do. Indeed, one of the strengths of this particular classification system might very well be that students at any level will be able to get the same results teachers do.

Many of our students exhibit what I've come to call the Clever-Hans syndrome. Clever-Hans for me goes back to Roger Brown's *Words and Things* [5] and reappears in *Pygmalion in the Classroom.* [6] Hans had become the most celebrated horse in Europe in the early 1900's because he apparently understood the spoken language and could answer questions by tapping the appropriate number of times with his hoof. After great initial fervor, the academic community learned the secret of Hans: watching closely, Hans would know he had tapped correctly as soon as his questioner unconsciously relaxed his tense, expectant posture. Similarly, students often attend to the teacher, not to the supposed substantive lesson, and react to matters of tone, not of fact.

The teacher says, for example, "Is *in* a preposition in the sentence: *He walked in?*"

"Well, the answer is 'No,'" the student reasons, "Not if you said it in that tone of voice."

A student can read the cue from his interrogator as Hans did from his. Perhaps students learn to study the teacher rather than the material because they've been deluded too often by traditional terms that say one thing to them but another to the teacher. As an example, consider the definition of the preposition which "shows the relation between one noun and another noun in a sentence." In "John loves Mary," one can claim that "love" is a preposition because it shows the relationship between one noun, "John," and another noun in the sentence, "Mary." Although the definition seems to permit this kind of interpretation, no teacher will accept it. The structuralist, with his carefully controlled definitional criteria, avoids that kind of problem entirely.

Now for both the traditional and the transformational grammar, I use the terms that are not overtly used in traditional grammar, "surface structure" and "deep structure," although it is amenable to the notions they represent. Thus the traditionalist will explain some element of the sentence on the basis of ellipses: *You* understood in imperative sentences, for example, and deletions in certain kinds of adverbial clauses:

*While swimming, he was attacked by a shark.*

The traditionalist has no qualms about supplying the phrase "he was":

*While he was swimming he was attacked by a shark.*

In a real sense, consequently, there's some connection shown between the superficial or surface forms and the underlying forms. It is the underlying form, of course, that conveys the meaning of that particular sentence. Now, as I indicate here, the difference between the components of surface structure and deep structure in the traditional versus the transformational account resides in the fact that the traditional grammarian did not have a systematic way of relating the two. There was no way of going directly from one to the other. In a transformational version, the deep structure is obtained through the phrase structure rules, to which transformational rules are applied to produce the surface forms. In short, there is a formal, an organized, a systematic way of dealing with the connections between deep structure and surface structure. The claim in the deep structure notion for the transformationalist is that here is where the meaning is obtained in any given sentence, the superficial form being obtained simply by applying transformations that do not change the meaning. What surprises me a great deal is that many teachers tend to assume that structural and transformational grammars are closely connected, or that they are connected more so than traditional and transformational grammars are. The reason for this may be due to the fact that articles in the *English Journal* and other professional periodicals often lump these grammars together as the "New English." They do not reveal that structural grammars are quite different from transformational grammars; nor do they show how, in fact, transformational grammars can be seen to be evolutionary from traditional grammars, from the kind of traditional grammar that the Port Royal grammarians of the 17th century have worked on.

The form of a transformational grammar, though the field is rapidly changing, may still be represented as follows:

## Figure 2

*F. Zidonis*

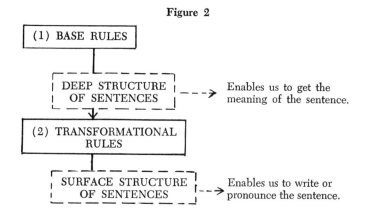

```
┌─────────────────┐
│ (1) BASE RULES  │
└─────────────────┘
        │
┌───────────────────┐
│ DEEP STRUCTURE    │ ──→  Enables us to get the
│ OF SENTENCES      │      meaning of the sentence.
└───────────────────┘
        │
┌───────────────────────┐
│ (2) TRANSFORMATIONAL  │
│      RULES            │
└───────────────────────┘
        │
┌───────────────────────┐
│ SURFACE STRUCTURE     │ ──→  Enables us to write or
│    OF SENTENCES       │      pronounce the sentence.
└───────────────────────┘
```

The movement now is towards making semantics a more central concern of language study, but the ways of achieving this goal are not at all clear at the present. In over-simplified fashion, Figure 2 shows that the transformational system has two components. One, the base rules or phrase structure rules, produces the deep structure of the sentence; the other component, transformational, acts on the products of the base to provide the surface forms that we utter or we see in print.

## Figure 3

Relationship Between Base Rules
and Tree Diagram

(A) BASE RULES (simplified)         (B) TREE DIAGRAM

1. S − −−→ Nom + VP
2. VP − − −→ Aux + V
3. V − − −→ Vtr + Nom
4. Aux − − −→ past
5. Nom − − → D + N
6. Vtr − − −→ Kiss . . .
7. D − − − → the . . .
8. N − − − → boy, girl, . . .

```
                    S
                   / \
              Nom      VP
             /|        / \
            D N    Aux   V
            |  |    |    / \
            |  |    |  Vtr  Nom
            |  |    |   |   /  \
            |  |    |   |  D    N
            |  |    |   |  |    |
          The boy  past kiss the girl
```

Figure 3 deals with the notion of diagramming in the transformational system. Reflect for a moment on the fact that traditional diagramming is entirely divorced from the grammatical system. The schema for traditional diagramming that is used most frequently by English teachers today is the one originated by Reed and Kellogg in the mid-nineteenth century. Nothing in the techniques used in traditional grammar indicates why any diagrams should be drawn, let alone this sort. In the transformational system there is a method of diagramming that I think has at least two advantages over that of the traditional account. First, there's a connection between the rules of the base and the eventual diagram (called "tree diagram," "tree," or "phrase marker"). Second, the phrase marker plays a role in helping establish whether certain transformations can be applied.

I have a set of base rules here in Figure 3 that are quite simplified. They differ a little from what you find in Paul Roberts, and also from what you find in the Ginn 7-10 Grammar by Roderick A. Jacobs and Peter S. Rosenbaum, who choose not to deal with phrase structure rules. If you have seen a set of rules of this sort, you know that the technique of definition is one of elaboration. An item introduced on the right side of the arrow will be further explained by other elaborations and succeeding rules until a final point is reached, the "terminal string," which is the underlying form of a sentence. It becomes a sentence in form when the appropriate transformations are applied. Rule 1 says that a sentence is rewritten as a NOM (Nominal) and a VP (Verb Phrase). The first step then in doing a phrase marker is to indicate that particular information with this pair of branches. NOM, according to Rule 5, is rewritten as a D (Determiner) plus N. Therefore the NOM in this tree diagram is shown to branch off into D and N. Hence there is a one-for-one connection between the rules in the base component and the tree, or phrase marker, that is a result of these. That's one advantage over the traditional account. Another is that the product of this phrase marker, the terminal string here, has a function in the rest of the grammar. It will show whether or not certain transformations apply to it; in effect, it establishes the domain of the transformation: either a particular string falls within the constraints of a given transformation which must therefore be applied, or else it does not and the transformation does not apply to that particular terminal string.

One of the claims made in the transformational version is that the diagram or phrase marker, which deals with the underlying deep structure of a sentence, provides us with the meaning of that sentence. Now there are some who are saying that we really ought to call that a semantic marker, for the meaning is obtained here. But notice how the diagram works in the three systems:

**Figure 4**

Three Diagrams for "The key opened the door."

(1) TRADITIONAL

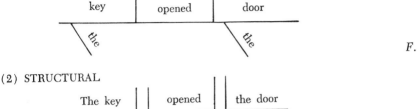

(2) STRUCTURAL

(3) TRANSFORMATIONAL

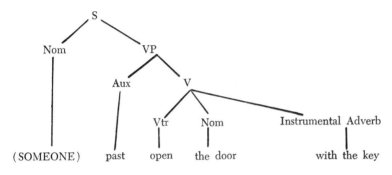

I think all of you would agree that this is the way this sentence would be represented in the traditional diagramming system. If we had used an adverb like "quietly" in any permissible location in the sentence, it would nevertheless be placed under "opened," for traditionally, we would say that it modifies the verb. In the structural diagram, however—under the immediate constituent analysis in which every utterance is cut into two parts until finally the ultimate constituents are reached—word order is kept inviolate. If "quietly" appeared in the sentence, the structuralist diagram would keep it wherever it appeared in the utterance. If it introduced the sentence, for example, then the first cut would be between it and the rest of the sentence, and "quietly" would probably be called a sentence modifier. If it appeared at the end, it would stay there and still receive that first cut. The point the structuralist exemplifies here is that word order in English is the most important grammatical feature and ought not to be ignored in the way that particular sentences or utterances are represented for further analysis.

To what extent does the diagram clarify the meaning of a sentence? The transformationalist claims that meanings are conveyed by the underlying forms of sentences, by their deep structure, which the phrase markers reveal. How does the native speaker understand a particular kind of sentence? What does he understand from so simple a sentence as "The key opened the door"? Note that for both traditionalist and structuralist the so-called complete subject is "the key" and the predicate is "opened the door," but the tree diagram reflects different underlying relationships. In no sense, of course, is the superficial subject the performer of the action signalled by the verb in this sentence: "the key" does not really "open" the door. For the agent used in this particular instance is not specified. Yet we understand, or we can assume, what that agent is. We know that someone opened the door and we know that the key is the instrument with which the door was opened and not the doer of the action. If this is really what we understand by the sentence, then there should be a representation of the sort that the transformational diagram depicts. For, presumably, the deep structure conveys the meaning of the sentence. What serves as the subject of the sentence in the surface structure can quite clearly be something else in its underlying form—an instrumental phrase in this example.

Examination of such shifts in case forms is now being carried on in transformational research, especially in Fillmore's "The Case for Case." [7] The term "case" indicates the semantic and syntactic relationship a noun has to its sentence. Consider these sentences, for example:

(1) Mother is cooking the potatoes.
(2) The potatoes are cooking.
(3) Mother is cooking.

*Mother* in this set of sentences would be the agentive case, that is, the animate doer of the action. *Potatoes* would be the objective case, the most neutral of cases. The relationships between *mother, is cooking,* and *potatoes* are the same in all three sentences, even though *potatoes* appears as the surface subject in (2) and is the deleted object in (3). Only an Alice-in-Wonderland sort of context would permit *potatoes* in (2) to serve as the animate performer of the action; and probably only a cannibalistic one permits *mother* in (3) to be taken as the objective case. Even though the surface forms of these sentences are different, then, it turns out that their underlying case relationships remain the same in all three versions.

It appears, furthermore, that nouns which are in different

cases cannot be conjoined, a fact lending support to the case analysis system developed by Fillmore. Consider the following sentences:

(1) John broke the window.
(2) A hammer broke the window.
(3) John broke the window with a hammer.

In this set, *John* is the agentive case, the animate doer of the action—we assume that he or someone like him wielded the hammer in (2) also; *window* is the objective case; and *hammer* is the instrumental case. Notice that we cannot conjoin agentive and instrumental to form this sentence:

(4) * John and a hammer broke the window.

Occasionally an ambiguity in a sentence can be clarified by classifying the object, by getting at the meaning of the object. The following unambiguous sentence has an ordinary object and permits the syntactically related question and answer:

(1) He is burning a *book*.
Q. What is he doing to the book?
A. What he is doing to the book is burning it.

In the following sentence, however, the syntactically related question is not permissible:

(2) He is writing a *book*.
Q. * What is he doing to the book?
A. * What he is doing to the book is writing it.

In (2) the object, *book*, does not come into existence until after the action of the verb is completed. Knowing whether the object exists before the action of the verb takes place thus helps determine how the sentence is to be interpreted. It pinpoints, for example, the ambiguity in this sentence:

(3) John paints nudes.

The object, *nudes*, has several meanings, but the question here is whether the objects John painted existed before or only after he did the painting. Is the object in (3) like that of (2) or like that of (1)? If (1), it might be termed an ordinary object; if (2), it is an "object of result," or what Lyons calls an "existential causative." [8] There is often a high degree of inter-dependence between a particular verb and a particular noun. This is a syntagmatic (as opposed to paradigmatic) interdependence, or presupposition, which helps in the analysis of vocabulary in a language—e.g., between verb and noun: bird/fly; fish/swim; adjective and noun: blond/hair; verb and ordinary object: drive/car; verb and noun instrumentally related: bite/teeth; kick/foot.

Attention to the lexicon involves a particular kind of grammatical information, I think. In general, it's true that there are two kinds of information about the language. We can consider generalizations about grammar as being the general knowledge of language; we can take information about individual words as specific knowledge of language. We have to know the syntax of a word—knowing the meaning, the semantic content of a word, isn't enough. On the other hand, being able to use a word in an appropriate syntactic location sometimes conflicts with the semantic load it carries. I'm reminded of that sixth grader's sentence—maybe you've seen this before:

> The fireman came out of the burning building *pregnant.* The dictionary entry for pregnant is *carrying a child:*
> The fireman came out of the burning building *carrying a child.*

Or again,

> He ate the *elite* of the pie.
> What is the *elite* of the pie? It is defined as *the best part.*

On the other hand, take those instances where the semantic load is similar, but where the syntactic environment is much different. *Averse* and *reluctant* mean pretty much the same thing, and yet they are used in complementary distribution:

| | | |
|---|---|---|
| reluctant groom | but not | * averse groom |
| reluctant to marry | but not | * averse to marry |
| averse to marriage | but not | * reluctant to marriage |
| averse to marrying | but not | * reluctant to marrying |

These syntactical constraints—this specific knowledge of the behavior of individual words—form part of the grammatical knowledge that's required before one can say he knows his language.

Let me turn finally to a schema dealing with the role of grammar in the language arts.

## Figure 5
### Grammar and the Language Arts

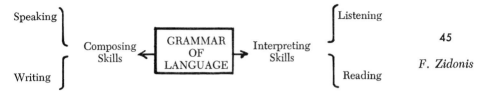

I don't really mean to put grammar in the center of curriculum, although the heading suggests this possibility. If grammar is conceived of as the attempt to explain how we are able to form sentences—novel sentences, almost effortlessly—how infants acquire language, how one interprets or is able to understand sentences, then it seems to me that the notion of grammar has been vastly expanded. It would include even the study of poetry. If one takes the four language arts—listening and reading, speaking and writing—one can think of them as being offshoots of two types of more basic skills: interpreting and composing. In terms of grammatical theory, the path one takes from deep structure to surface grammar involves composing skills. When one starts with surface structure, one is involved with interpreting skills: listening or reading. Students have to know what the relations of sentence elements are. But clues to these relationships are given only in surface structures which the intuitively astute reader, of poetry or of prose, is able to solve. He may not be conscious of what it is he does when he achieves this particular feat. But it seems to me that a great many students would be better readers of literature if they were taught to move more fluently between surface and deep structures. For example, here's a couplet from Browning that is puzzling unless the syntax is sorted out:

> Irks care the crop-full bird?
> Frets doubt the maw-crammed beast?

Unless the reader can see the connection between the subject and the verb—having first sorted those elements out—he will not understand these strings of fairly simple words. Only when the reader recognizes that *care* and *doubt* are subjects, not verbs, does the meaning of the above sentences become clear. The more usual way of framing those questions would be as follows:

> Does care irk the crop-full bird?
> Does doubt fret the maw-crammed beast?

I'm suggesting simply that what a great number of sophisticated and intuitively skilled readers do needs to be examined some-what more carefully for the unsophisticated reader. These reading techniques don't come automatically to fifth, seventh, and ninth graders. There is value in the kind of paraphrase that this search for the deep structure quite often involves.

There is considerable grammatical information that comes into play in the response to a poem or a sentence. Let me conclude with this four-line poem from Herrick. Ordinarily a poem should be presented in its entirety, since it is organic, but I want to look at the image that the poem presents line by line. The title is "Upon a Child":

*(1) Here a pretty baby lies,*
It is possible to be specific about every item in the line—to draw features for specified location or unspecified location, or to talk about the connections between an adjective like *pretty* and the sorts of nouns it can appear with. But at this point let's just say that *here* is an unspecified location and that "a pretty baby" conjures a pleasant kind of image.

*(2) Sung asleep with lullabies;*
The construction "with lullabies" is an adverbial one that indicates a causal connection with the preceding line: the singing of lullabies has put the baby to sleep.

*(3) Pray be silent and not stir*
This line indicates, I think, that we're perhaps at the side of the crib in which the baby is sleeping. The verb *stir* seems to be an intransitive or reflexive-transitive: "do not stir yourself." This notion is compatible with that of being silent.

*(4) Th' easy earth that covers her.*
This dramatically ironic line now completely changes the image of the first three lines. The pivotal word is the verb *stir:* it turns out to be an ordinary sort of transitive. The poem here becomes specified. Whereas we thought we were at a crib side with the baby asleep, we are instead evidently at the site of the grave. "Sung asleep with lullabies" is not causally related to the baby's lying here, but is seen as commentary or accompaniment now. And "Pray be silent and not stir" need no longer be read as a single, repeated plea for silence but possibly as three separate commands: *Pray, Be Silent, and (Do) Not Stir.*

There is, in short, a lot of grammatical information involved in obtaining the meaning even from simple-looking lines. And careful attention must be given to syntax if their meaning is to be derived.

1. Noam Chomsky, "A Review of B. F. Skinner's *Verbal Behavior*," *Language* 35 (1959), pp. 26-59. Reprinted by permission of the Linguistic Society of America.

2. Paul Roberts, *Patterns of English* (New York: Harcourt Brace Jovanovich, Inc., 1956).

3. Charles Carpenter Fries, *American English Grammar* (New York: Appleton-Century-Crofts, 1940).

4. —————, *Structure of English* (New York: Harcourt Brace Jovanovich, Inc., 1952).

5. Roger Brown, *Words and Things* (Glencoe, Illinois: The Free Press, 1958) Chapter II, pp. 57-80.

6. Robert Rosenthal and Lenore Jacobson, *Pygmalion in the Classroom* (New York: Holt, Rinehart and Winston, Inc., 1968).

7. Charles J. Fillmore, "The Case for Case," *Universals in Linguistic Theory*, ed. Emmon Bach and R. T. Harms (New York: Holt, Rinehart & Winston, Inc., 1968).

8. John Lyons, *Introduction to Theoretical Linguistics* (London: Cambridge University Press, 1968), p. 439.

*Behavioral science is prepared to make to contributions from the point of view of our concern with language. Its first contribution has to do with the way we look at language, a way that can be productive and profitable and extremely useful. And second, it has things to say about how we go about teaching some of the goals we establish in our language instruction programs.*

# Language: A Challenge

## by Stanley M. Sapon

The title, "Language: A Challenge," affords me the opportunity to offer challenges, or challenge a notion of language. Most get-togethers of people who share common professional interests are generally characterized by an awful lot of agreement about issues, some of which are much too painful or fierce to shake up, and so we let our sleeping issues lie and we talk with great confidence about the things we know very well and about the problems with whose existence we are equally familiar. But I think reaching for things that are not ordinarily touched upon represents one of my central objectives.

**Dr. Stanley M. Sapon**
Professor of Psycholinguistics
Department of Languages and Linguistics
University of Rochester

My joint appointment in psychology and languages and linguistics is a kind of end result of a whole series of "non-success" experiences. I really began with a dual job—that of a linguist and a foreign language teacher. It turned out to be not too difficult and extremely enjoyable to follow the tasks described in the manual for what a linguist is supposed to do. It wasn't quite so enjoyable and it wasn't quite so easy to confront the tasks of a foreign language teacher. One of the first things, of course, that you run across in foreign language teaching—and I suppose the teaching of English has got something in common with this as well—is the specification of what we're setting out to teach, the agreement on how we're going to test, how successful we've been in our teaching, and a final accommodation between how successful we've been in what we actually *achieved* and how much we actually *set out to achieve*. This kind of an accommodation generally appears in regularly revised curricula and new flights of syllabus fancy. It's a pretty uncomfortable spot to be in and I'm not going to flagellate the English teachers, but I'm going to have at the foreign language teachers because I can do that without fear of retribution.

The kind of thing that I found profoundly disturbing was the kind of violent mismatch between the reason for teaching foreign languages and what we were actually expected to teach, and then what we were actually testing for in our final examination. So we got into this kind of situation: FL teaching was supposed to be some sort of "new key" which said we were going to make FL teaching relevant; we were going to break out of the traditional mold that Latin translation, etc., had locked us up in; we were going to make FL teaching a fresh, new, relevant approach; and the aural-oral method was discovered and was really a fresh, new, exciting discovery about on the par with the "rediscovery" of natural childbirth. My goodness gracious, what a fantastic revelation in the 20th century! As a matter of fact, both these revelations reached a kind of height of popularity about the same time. Natural childbirth has fared better than FL teaching. But in the FL field we "rediscovered" the aural-oral approach, and we were going to teach our young people to really speak the foreign language, function in the foreign language, and if we had to, sacrifice some of the traditional methods. And then I ran into real conflict because I took these new notions very seriously and set out to teach my students (I was teaching Spanish) to *really perform* in Spanish, to be able to speak Spanish sentences that could be understood by other Spanish speakers.

Well, the first thing that happened, of course, was the recognition that if they were going to perform in these two areas successfully, they couldn't do this successfully on a limitless scale. I wasn't going to be able to expect my students at the end of two semesters of college work to be able to say everything that was sayable in Spanish by people who'd reached the age of 22 or 30 in a Spanish-speaking country. Nor could I expect them to understand everything that might conceivably be said by a Spanish speaker. We had set our sights for excellence and performance and it turned out that we had to lower our sights in terms of quantity, that we couldn't have the *quality* we promised with the kind of *quantity* that had been implied in the old style of teaching.

I constructed a course, the objective of which was 90% achievement for 90% of the students on 90% of the subject matter. And I really achieved it. I offered it to my colleagues, stood back, humbly bowed my head, and waited for the accolades. Instead I got the axe. They said, "Well sure, they pronounce Spanish beautifully, but they only have 500 words and what kind of an achievement is that for a whole year's work? A vocabulary of 500 words! Using our old standard textbook, the students learned 500 words in four weeks. What is this nonsense of 500 words for a whole year?" And then I said, "Yes, you actually covered 2000 words in a year, but how many of those 2000 words could you call for at any given time; how many do you expect to get back and with what reliability? Now here we have 500 words, which I offer with 90% reliability in 90% of the students 90% of the time."

And then we discovered that people had been really offering a kind of lip-service to the aural-oral approach as long as it was not available, but when it was available, we discovered that there were many, many other aspects of FL instruction that my intensive little course overlooked completely. There were so many, many things untouched. In fact, some of the "real reasons" for studying foreign language I had overlooked and omitted in my course.

I had naively assumed that the reason for studying a FL was to achieve some honest skill in performing it, and I discovered to my chagrin how badly I had misread the directives. It turned out, for example, that there was nothing about Spanish culture in my course, that in spite of the high fluency in a limited range that my students had, they didn't know anything about how boys and girls walk counter-clockwise in the park and forms of courtship behavior in some Spanish-speaking countries. This was seen as evidence of a lack of training in Spanish. My students, for example, did not know the name of Don Quixote's broken-down nag, nor did they know the name of the gallant steed of El Cid. As a matter of fact, there were a number of horses' names they didn't know. And this was taken as a lack of breadth in Spanish culture.

We discovered also that my students didn't know anything about grammar. Namely, when asked to talk *about* the Spanish language, one found them singularly inarticulate . . . there wasn't much they could say about it. An English equivalent of this would be exactly what happened in one case. One of my students was chided in a subsequent class for not knowing what a condition contrary to fact was. He came back to me to berate me because I had failed to teach him that. I spoke to him in Spanish and said "You know that." And he said "si supiera lo que quiere decir, no se lo preguntaria!" (If I knew what it meant, I wouldn't ask you!) This poor fellow did not "know" what a condition contrary to fact was.

I finally took a look at the disaster that I had accomplished, and identified it as what I call now, I guess, a kind of transposition of the "Finian's Rainbow" Syndrome into the language teaching world.

There is a little character in the play who describes his love-life in simple terms. He says, "If I'm not near the one I love, I love the one I'm near." An extremely satisfying situation. You can't possibly go wrong on it. And the FL situation has pretty much worked itself into that same thing. We found in the list of reasons for FL instruction long, long lists of intriguing and impressive and interesting goals which were Finian's Rainbow items. Items which said, in essence, "If I can't teach the things that I think are important, I will consider important those things that I can teach." It works out pretty well.

Teaching oral performance is difficult. Teaching people the names of famous horses, that's a snap. Teaching them that El Greco was not really a Spanish painter and that he was so named because he came from Greece and that he painted moody landscapes, that would be easy. Art and artists became part of the "real reason" for studying foreign languages. Geography—principal products, main exports, dating behavior, art, curious anecdotes—all these things are easily teachable. These are the aspects of foreign language instruction that will mostly be carried out in English. We talk about the culture of the foreign country in English. The teacher teaches them to draw the flag and coins, and a whole realm of things totally alien to show them that "Yes, Virginia, there are Spanish-speaking people in the world, and there's the money they spend to prove it." Grammar, the ability to talk *about* the language, is teachable, and the teaching plays an essential part. And now I think we can begin to read somewhat into our own concerns in the field of English.

The teaching of grammar came to be esteemed on at least

two grounds: first, that it was important in its own right. Grammar was considered to be universal, so if you taught the student at least the grammar of his own language and provided him with the ability to make statements *about* English in a very special vocabulary, you not only enhanced his *performance* in English—in the words of the "Laugh-In" character, "He'll be a better man for that"—but also even satisfied the Puritan Ethic, to the extent that it hurt so much it must certainly be very good for him. Well, we got that out of grammar. Second, it also prepared one for excellent functioning in a foreign language setting, so much so that—you probably know this, as English specialists—one of the principal reasons for the consistent record of less than valiant performance in FL instruction for years has been the fault of the English teachers. Constantly you hear this complaint: "How can you teach these people Spanish when they don't even know *English* grammar?" "They wouldn't know a subjunctive if they sat on one." "It's dreadful! How can they expect us to teach you kids Spanish when you don't know English grammar at all."

That turns out to have been an honest escape hatch to the extent that much of the approach to learning Spanish or any other language was via a translation of the structure of the new language into a kind of Latinic type of structure, then "regressed" back into English terms. That was the devious way we got students to speak and perform in the foreign language. The fact that it didn't work very well was not taken as any evidence of something lacking with regard to procedure. It just meant that other people were just not preparing the students adequately for this. But the grammar became an important part in and of itself as well as a means of entry or access to the kind of performance that was really to be esteemed or really to be reached for.

The literature of the language in question became a multiple-purpose end-goal for FL instruction. Literature—and I've been at this thing for ten or twelve years now and have yet to figure it out—is both the reason or justification *for* learning the FL and the way *through which* you acquire skill in the FL. There's something about that that has a kind of "lift-yourself-by-your-own-bootstraps" flavor. It is difficult to see how something can be both a means and an end in and of itself, how it can function as a procedure whereby you become a skilled performer in the literature, starting at some low level of ability, and of course, the terminal skill is what justifies the existence of the subject matter in the curriculum.

The issue of justifying the subject matter in the curriculum is something that we haven't often looked at. On the college scene, particularly, we find something interesting going on. There are two levels of performance in the college departments of foreign language and literature. There's the "high-level" performance, the kind that is esteemed and admired and appreciated, the performance that yields, in the last analysis, the appreciation of your colleagues, raises, promotions, and something really publishable, and that's literary criticism. And then there's the other half of the department, the kind you'd rather not talk about; it's the donkey work. It's this business of teaching the little parrots or little monkeys to see and do. Naturally, a totally "non-academic" and "non-intellectual" piece of behavior is what is asked for; it just happened to be a necessary evil that no one could read French literature in French until they had gone through a certain period of time in acquiring these non-valued behaviors of reading French. The literature as the target in this case provided the justification and a kind of freedom from guilt or some semblance of professionalism for the person whose only responsibility was the target of establishing simple kinds of FL behavior in students. If it weren't for literature at the other end to provide the dignity, there'd be no reason to continue. That's the kind of snarl that FL teaching has found itself in and still is in to a large extent.

We have an interesting thing on the horizon in a number of universities. We have at Rochester, for example, a system that is used by a half-dozen other places in the country. We made a split, and foreign literature is now in a department of its own. That would have left language teaching in a department of its own and that, of course, was a fate too horrible to even consider. How can you have a college department with people with professorial rank and things like that dedicating their lives to teaching . . . donkeys? Meaningless movements of the jaw, tongue and lips, etc. We got out of that one. My department is the department that is responsible for teaching languages, so the literature people now have the department of foreign and comparative literature in another building where they live in shining virtue and professional achievement. But we're not without some saving grace because our department also has, finally, an academic and intellectually respectable subject to teach— linguistics. It's the Department of Languages *and* Linguistics. And I am not really quite sure at this stage of the game whether linguistics is any more relevant to language teaching than literature was.

I'm trying to give you some background of the kind of concerns that I have had as a language teacher and the kind of confrontation that came to me when I was charged with the responsibility of designing a programmed course in Spanish.

And I've talked a little bit about how I was punished for my achievement. But it had some good things in the sense that it made me confront, for the first time, some of the issues of language in a brand new way. And it was these first steps, I think, that took me across the hall into psychology.

Programmed instruction, by its very nature, assumes that you have something to teach that is measurable. The only way you can possibly know if you've done something is if you have some means of measuring it. To have something measurable, you must have something specifiable. If you have something specifiable, presumably you are also touching on things that are relevant. And so the first brush with programmed instruction brought the notion of coming up with a series of relevant, measurable objectives. Another something that the FL field hadn't brushed with, I don't think, really seriously before, is that an awful lot of words that you use to describe the performance turned out to be not measurable and when proponents of these valued objectives were pressed hard for possible measures of these valued objectives, they got angry, and accused me of being irreverent and irritating on purpose. So that when someone says one of the first things that we expect to have out of this course of study is that the students will demonstrate "an appreciation of X," write that down. Because I went out to survey the field to try and find out what I was supposed to do. "How will I know he is 'appreciating' X?" One of the reasons for studying is how he "feels" about the foreign culture. He's got to appreciate it, understand it, and he must have insights into it; that's reasonable. All right, how will I know that he has reached the objective? How will I know that he indeed does "appreciate" and "understand" and "see into"? Tell me how I will know this.

When I asked these questions, people began to get squirmy and uncomfortable and sat sideways and then began to get a little angry at me because I was prodding and pushing, and finally I got put down once and for all—"You're not much of a Spanish teacher, are you? Because if you were a really good Spanish teacher, you wouldn't ask me how you could tell when a student appreciates. You'd know it. You'd just kind of feel it; you'd sense it. You can tell by just looking at students that you've been working with for a whole semester whether they really appreciate this," and so on. I said, "Oh well, I confess my failure there." I suggested I wasn't a good Spanish teacher because I didn't *know*, just by looking at my students; and I wasn't getting much help from my colleagues who insisted that objectives like this were part of the course.

The quest for relevance, and of course, that's one of the words that are critical too—*relevant* and *measurable* objectives

—was a kind of solid, propelling force toward a tight, careful analysis of what we were really doing. Some of it was meaningless noise that we emitted under spurious camaraderie and co-professionalism that we all knew to be undefinable. And the students agreed to play along with the game and made equivalent noises. Some of it was real; some of it was very relevant; some of it was very measurable. We found that people could indeed be led to produce many of these terminal behaviors that were declared to be valid. We still had the task ahead of us of persuading the rest of the world who originally asked for them that they had what they ordered, that it was good to look upon. Now, that battle is still going on.

But by way of background in the discussion, these are the kinds of challenges that we are making now, that took me into a new field, accurately called the "experimental analysis of verbal behavior," sometimes referred to as "operant conditioning." I don't like the term "operant conditioning" because it supplies a direct verbal link with Pavlovian conditioning and conjures up visions of salivating dogs and ringing bells and a punishment effect. I think the one magic word here is "operant."

I want now to reach for a quick capsule description of the science of the experimental analysis of behavior. We're going to discuss what it means in terms of language and the kinds of relevance I think it has for us with our concern for all sorts of levels of English teaching and learning—including those people who are concerned with English as a second language, those who are concerned with English in an honestly bi-lingual situation, those who are concerned with social dialects and the problems involved in crossing them in school settings, and the like.

The capsule definition is that the experimental analysis of behavior is a way of looking at behavior, anybody's behavior, any organism's behavior as that behavior which serves to change the environment of the organism that emits the behavior. We are concerned with, as we said before, what is known as operant behavior. Operant behavior is the behavior through which an organism operates or acts on his environment. And it is one way of looking at behavior, not in terms of the form or shape of the behavior itself, but rather, how it is that the behavior emitted by an organism changes his environment.

The simplest example would be the behavior of picking up a glass, holding it under the spigot at the sink, turning the tap, filling the glass with water. Now, in that little string of behaviors we have watched somebody act upon his environment. The environment before he approached the sink was the environment in which drinking water was not immediately present and available. Then we got a whole string of behaviors with the arms and legs and hands in the presence of the sink and the drinking glass and now the environment has changed because, lo and behold, drinking water is on the scene. This is a case of acting on the environment.

Someone who is in the room and opens the door changes his environment to the extent that now he has access to another space. And, of course, when he uses his legs to transport himself across the threshold, he has changed his environment again. He's acted upon his environment. He now confronts another bit of three-dimensional space. Reaching for stairs, sitting, standing, walking, feeding ourselves, all the countless tasks that we see are clearly on the motor level, are great examples of operant behavior.

Part of the interesting thing, however, comes out of looking at this behavior—we said that it was an *analysis* of behavior; all I said was that we simply agreed to talk about behavior in a special way and about how an organism acts upon his environment. The special thing happens when we say "We're going to look at this behavior in terms of a three-term analysis model." What we are saying now is—there's a kind of Aristotelian balance here—that every event has a beginning, a middle, and an end.

Suppose we look at this behavior—for example, we see a man at a water cooler. He has just stepped on the foot pedal and we see him drinking water. The behavior in question, or what's been happening here, is that the man stepped on a foot pedal. We've actually just described the middle. What we really need to say is we have here a behavioral event—stepping on a foot pedal—that takes place in the presence of a certain setting. It takes place on the occasion of his having been without water, on the occasion of being in the presence of a water cooler. And then we have the most important thing of all perhaps: the consequence of that behavior. The consequence of stepping on the foot pedal is a mouthful of water. And by looking at every behavioral event in those three terms, we have the chance to take something that might ordinarily be considered a one-piece affair and look at it in terms of three component parts, each of which is available for separate study, analysis and change.

If we were to watch this fellow approach the water cooler, press the pedal, and see no water appear, we would be able to predict that the frequency of his coming back to the water cooler and pressing the pedal is going to be slightly lower, not quite so highly probable. We won't say that it is not going to happen, but it has decreased a wee bit in probability. He comes back to the water cooler again several hours later and steps on the pedal and no water comes out. We have just seen something else happen to shift the probability. If he comes back to the water cooler 4, 5, 6 times in the course of a week and water does not appear, we're in a position now to make even stronger statements about the probability. That water cooler, in essence, is beginning to "disappear" from his environment: the presence of the water cooler, which was the occasion for coming up and stepping on the pedal, is now beginning to drop out. If we have, on the other hand, a situation in which water *does* appear when he steps on the pedal, we can say now that given a condition of thirst, and the presence of the water cooler that dispenses water, there's going to be a high probability of his approaching the water cooler and stepping on the pedal.

We can, in a way, now change the probability of somebody's stepping on the pedal of the water cooler simply by controlling our switch the way you might see someone do on "Candid Camera"—make the water cooler operative or non-operative. And you can change the probabilities of approaching or not approaching a given piece of apparatus.

The water cooler itself and a given period of time without liquid, or a given level of salinity in the blood, are also necessary conditions for stepping on the pedal. As we said before, you cannot step on the pedal if it's not there. The likelihood of stepping on the pedal is increased by a level of water deprivation over a period of time.

We talked about *consequences* in terms of the appearance of water or the non-appearance of water. We can talk about the first term, which is the *stimulus setting* or the occasion for the behavior to take place, in terms of the presence of the water cooler. We talk about the *behavior* as simply those muscle movements involved in stepping on the foot pedal. This is a piece of operant behavior that can be described in terms of these three very discrete phases: 1. the stimulus setting; 2. the behavior; 3. the consequences.

Now this is a really very simple—oversimplified, if you will— accurate, though perhaps not very persuasive statement of what is the essence of a science. The question is what can we do with it and where does it lead us? What have I been doing with it and what has it done for me?

I can say two things. Behavioral science is prepared to make two contributions from the point of view of our concern with language. Its first contribution has to do with the way we can look at language, a way that can be productive and profitable and extremely useful. And second, it has things to say about how we go about teaching some of the goals we establish in our language instruction programs.

S. Sapon

Let's come back to the first contribution. What we're talking about today is the issue of how it helps us see language in a slightly different fashion. The laboratory in which I work has got a special name on the door, and it's not called a "Language Laboratory" or "Linguistics Laboratory"; it's called the "Verbal Behavior Laboratory." And that's the first tip-off as to what is so different about the approach. We said before that we were talking about behavior and the analysis of behavior and our concern with looking at behavior through the lens of the three-term contingency model. And this could make some clear and obvious sense when we talk about opening doors and operating a water cooler and driving cars and moving the world around physically, with our hands and feet, and so on. The question is, "What does this have to do with language?" Before I begin the answer, I would like to avoid the term "language" for a while and talk instead about "verbal behavior."

I prefer the term "verbal behavior" to "language" for a number of reasons. First, the term "language," which I lived with for a long, long time, and at one time actually considered to be the subject matter of my professional specialty . . . language is a *thing*. I see textbooks on the shelves which read "Using Your Language," "Language Is a Tool," "Language Is a Gift," and "language is something that man has been given and no other creature has," so it's a tool, a thing, a gift, a possession. It's something that people strive to "put into" another person. And this distresses me because it conjures up a kind of strange pedagogical image of students being a kind of a sack into which educators seek to pour good things.

We know we're educators because we know what we've poured into the sack. Unfortunately, these sacks differ, because some sacks apparently have no bottoms and the little things we pour in run right out. There are some sacks that apparently hold what we pour in but never give it back. We know it's in there because we put it in but we can't seem to get it out. And that's not really a successful teaching venture. But as I say, I find this image distressing. It is also misleading and non-productive. And looking at language as a thing or a tool does not really open any magical doors, from an educational standpoint, since we really don't know how to make any meaningful pedagogical sense out of such things as "giving a child a tool" and then "teaching him how to use the tool." These are metaphorically delightful statements, but in a practical sense, they're sheer nonsense.

I give a child a saw. Here it is. Look at it. I'm going to teach you how to use it. First, I'm going to see that he holds it in his hand. Now I'm going to teach him how to move his hand with the saw in his hand. But this metaphorical approach to language does not really lead to new and useful pedagogical implementation.

We don't know how to *give* a child language. It doesn't come in capsule form or liquid form; it cannot be injected hypodermically. There is no medium through which one can instill, inject, place *into* an organism what is actually not a thing, but rather *a special way of behaving.*

If you look at a child who is reported or seen to have "high-level language skills" and contrast him with a child who has "poor language skills," I, as a behavioral scientist, would ask, "How can you tell the difference between the two children?" And you will tell me immediately, "Just watch. Watch what this one does in a certain setting and watch what this one does not do in the same setting." And then, of course, I'm getting very happy because we're getting really close to honest descriptions that we're all likely to use because you're telling me now about things he *does.* You're telling me something about his *behavior* and we do, indeed, have scientific and pedagogical procedures, techniques for doing something about the way people behave.

There's not a thing we can do about somebody's *attitudes;* all we can change, perhaps, is the way he *behaves.* If this child has "a good attitude" toward his studies and this child has "a bad attitude" toward his studies and we ask the question "How can you tell the difference?" and you answer that the child who has the "good attitude" behaves in the following way . . . and the child with the "bad attitude" behaves in the following way . . . , then the object of our instruction shall *not* be to change his attitudes, but rather, to change the way in which he *behaves.*

We are well supplied with terms like "attitude" and "motivation." They're interesting and they seem to have some explanatory effect, but they don't really touch what we're trying to do. There are no devices for molding these invisible essences inside of people. But we sure as heck can put our hands or our eyeballs on behavior that the children emit. And talking about "verbal behavior" rather than "language" means we are talking about the kinds of things people do with their mouths and their faces and their fingers. Now that's something we can touch directly.

If we can find people who can specify, for example, what a good and viable and necessary and esteemed piece of verbal behavior is, then we have a kind of pedagogical target that we're likely to be able to reach. The simple act of defining and describing it and setting it in the kind of framework that permits looking at it as behavior brings us more than halfway to the task of being able to establish it. And, of course, establishing a new behavior in a child is a kind of technical way of talking about "teaching something to the child."

But you'll notice that we've departed from the image of the sack because if we're talking about establishing a new behavior in a child, and the child does, indeed, emit this new behavior, then we know we've made it. If he doesn't emit the new behavior, *we* have not yet made it. This is not quite the same thing as saying, "I taught him all about bipeds and quadrupeds, but he doesn't remember it." If the object of the game is getting a response to "What's a quadruped?" the response should be "A four-legged animal." "Give me an example." "A cat." "What's a biped?" etc. If he gives you an example, you know you've made it. That's simple. It's not quite the same thing as saying, "I taught him and he didn't learn." We have a definition now that says that "there is no teaching without learning." There are *attempts* at teaching, but we've only made it when we've finished it. Our tests can be useful if we look at things in the same general operant framework.

We talked about a three-term contingency model, that is, looking at behavior in terms of the occasion on which it is being emitted, the behavior itself, and the consequences of that behavior. Now the middle term, from the point of view of students of language, is likely to be the one that is talked about almost exclusively. If we had the sentence "Would you be kind enough to open the door for me?", that's what might be written down and subjected to analysis. We'd be looking at the *shape and form* of what somebody said. This is the subject matter of linguistics, generally speaking—the form and structure, *the middle term.* Some attention is paid to the occasions, the settings, the kinds of stimulus settings in which behavior is emitted; rarely, but it's there sometimes. *Practically none is paid to its consequences!*

No one ever asks in linguistic analysis, "What happened to the fellow after he said this?" The real focus of interest is on the form or shape of the response itself. This is very different from the kind of approach that involves function.

Here is an example of the kind of things that happen when we look at form and function together and we look at a piece of verbal behavior, looking carefully at just the first two terms, namely, the occasion for the behavior and the shape of the behavior itself.

If I were to tell you that my little girl said to me today "Four," I wouldn't see any signs of enthusiasm or excitement. Someone says to me, "Well, how old is she?" I say, "Let me tell you something else she said. I said, 'How old are you?' and then she said, 'Four.' And that's right." It doesn't sound like a magnificent achievement, though. I held up four fingers and said, "How many fingers am I holding up?" And she said "Four." That's pretty good. I said to her, "How many legs does a rhinoceros have?" She said "Four." I said, "According to the ancient Greeks, how many humours were there in the human body?" She said "Four." "According to Einstein and Lorenz, how many dimensions are there?" She said "Four." This kid is getting smarter by the minute!

What we have here, in essence, is the subtle transfer from a preschool setting to an advanced university level in theoretical physics. And yet the shape and form of the response, the verbal behavior, in every case, in and of itself, written down, would be exactly the same. And I offer you, for fun, the challenge of providing really interesting and exciting and thought-provoking questions that yield the answer "Four." But we have here a case in which the shape of the behavior itself is no different from the preschool level through the university level. What *has* changed is the stimulus setting, the stimulus control, the occasion for the emission of the specific piece of behavior.

S. *Sapon*

*Education is a transaction in which the teacher "leads out" from the child's belief system; it is also a transaction in which the child, particularly the child who comes from a culture or neighborhood different from the teacher's, can potentially "lead" the teacher "out" from her belief system.*

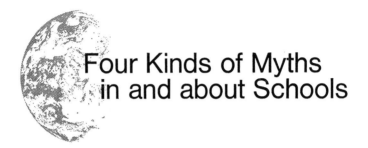

# Four Kinds of Myths in and about Schools

## by Paul A. Olson

There are four kinds of belief systems, or myths, which affect the process of education. The first is made up of myths which prevail in the culture of the home, the beliefs which the child picks up from his mother and father. The second kind involves the system of beliefs which "controls" what happens in the classroom; a classroom is a projection of the "system." Actually, the "system" is only the adult culture which controls education, an adult culture projected into the rooms in which kids are expected to learn. The third kind of belief (or myth) system is that which kids elaborate for themselves in their play and in their acting out: their intergroup reactions with one another, with adult culture, and with the "system." The final kind of myth is that taught in mythology courses.

The "myths" which I am going to be talking about are nar-

Dr. Paul A. Olson
Professor of English
University of Nebraska

ratives expected to have some significant effect on the behavior of people: on the way in which they see the world or the way in which they act upon it. Such narratives are in part reflections of the real world in which people find themselves, but they are also more. Odysseus' fabulous journeys in the *Odyssey* come from *two* real worlds: the world of the archaic culture of the seventh century B.C., when Homer lived, and the world of the culture of the eleventh century B.C., which actually engaged in the Trojan wars. But there is a deeper sense in which the story of Odysseus' journey comes from two worlds—the world of the actual and the world of rehearsal. Polyphemus is a picture-fantasy of what we fear when self-interest is unleashed and grows large apart from a civic sense; he is also a reflection at a distance of the view of life of the anarchic philosophers. Odyssean myth is not simply a phantasized reflection of what one finds around one. It is a projection, a translation of an *idea* into a verbal emblem, an eidolon. (The word eidolon as I use it comes out of Tasso, who suggests that poets make "idols" in the benign sense: pictures which are Yeats' "self form mockers of man's enterprise.") The pictures, in turn, represent ideal forms of life, ideal states toward which man aspires, or demonic and perfectly hideous states from which man seeks to escape. For instance, a modern musical comedy is a kind of effort to present an "idol" of what love ought to be; perhaps Frankenstein is a picture of that mechanical lovelessness from which we are trying to escape.

The myths—the neither true nor true-seeming narratives which we construct—tend to work at two levels. Most fantastic stories do. If someone tells a dirty joke at a cocktail party, he will partly tell it for its entertainment value and partly for its point. When someone listens to the story, he may indicate with his gestures and his eyes that he gets, or doesn't get, the point of the story. And this may be independent of his laughing. The dirty story is usually somewhat fantastic whenever it makes a "comment." Generally mythic stories—the kinds of stories which I have been talking about—tend also to be fantastic and to entertain, but their "fantasticalness" communicates a point. They entertain by communicating a point figuratively and through conventional, culture-bound symbolism. Such stories tend to be, for the most part, on their mimetic surfaces, creatures of the imagination alone; there is some absolute difference between the stories and life as we actually see it. *The stories lie.*

Now the question of the poet's mythic lie was perhaps first raised by Plato when he asked whether poets ought not to be exiled from the Republic as being liars. Plato's question is not such a dumb question as modern critics would make it. For it asks, "Well, what are false stories for?" If they are lies on the surface, what are they for? Generally the answer has been the allegorist's answer and not Plato's—that the poets, dreamers, and the pornographer's lies are all allegories, designed to make men into different sorts of creatures. Somehow beneath the surface of the fantastic story lies the figurative meaning—the point of the story—which tells what we ought to do or where we ought to go. The ethical question is not "Does the man lie on the surface?" but "What kind of person is this sort of 'lie'—this fiction—calculated to bring into being?" Many Biblical stories, many classical stories, and much of the poetry of the Middle Ages have been read as allegories for centuries. I would like to suggest that the dreams that kids dream, the stories that they themselves tell, and many of the fantastic dreams in which we ourselves indulge are allegories of our enterprise—allegories of what we want to be and what we would like for our children. Hence my lecture makes no absolute distinction between the myths of the home, the child, the school, and the myths of other cultures.

I. **The Myths of the Home and the School:** The process of education is a lot of things. One of the things which is constantly taking place in the process is the effort *to lead a man from one state to another;* such an effort says to a man or to a woman or to a child, "Where *you* are isn't where other people think you need to be; where you, in your own mind, think you ought to be; or where nature would have you be were nature allowed to flourish in the best of circumstances." If leading weren't our purpose, we wouldn't have schools. Every time we begin the process of education, we raise the question, "Where are we leading and from what point are we leading?" Whenever we engage in the process we must have some implicit or explicit conception of an ideal state to which we lead and a demonic state from which we flee. But we sometimes forget that those children whom we lead and their parents also have conceptions of ideal and demonic states. Sometimes their conceptions have little to do with ours: the conceptions of where man goes to become fully human which the schools impose and the conceptions which Navaho Indians or followers of Malcolm X have of where a child ought to be "led" are different.

How do we mediate between the old and the new in mythoi, between the conservative and the radical? Traditionally, when a new group emerges, one of the first things that it does is to create a new mythology. It might be argued that its emergence is marked by its creation of a mythos. I suppose that the hippies and the yippies are in the process of creating a new mythology for many Americans. The fact that they live in groups, the fact that the things they do are done in groups, and that they share a set of ideas and narratives, is what makes them so threatening to most of us. For as soon as a new story or a new set of stories emerges, a set which really implies action, the culture in which the new story appears experiences a kind of crisis over the question of what the old stories ought to mean. Yippie and hippie poetry and hippie and beat novels appropriate Zen Buddhism and traditional Buddhism and traditional Christianity to new purposes. Much of the traditional imagery of Christianity has been Buddhism taken over and made new in the poetry of the Plaths, the Ginzbergs, and the rock writers; some of the traditional icons of conventional bourgeois society in America have been stolen and put to an entirely different purpose by the "new left" (i.e., the Santa Claus suit that Jerry Rubin wore when he appeared before the House Un-American Activities Committee. Rubin took over American myth to say something about the functions of the House Un-American Activities Committee). We experienced a similar kind of trauma when Darwin gave us a new story of creation, and the Biblical story had to be "translated." What I am going to be talking about is the process of translation and appropriation—the conflicts which exist between the stories which kids from outsider's groups and from many quite square groups are telling and the stories which our education system is telling.

Before I do that, let me specify what I mean by appropriating or translating narratives which are central in a belief system. The process of appropriating narratives is a process concerning which people have been self-conscious for a long time. The Church fathers faced the problem in the form of pagan myth and learning; St. Augustine and other church fathers well-educated in Roman tradition wished to preserve some of the Rome which they knew. As proud Romans, they did not leave their civilization behind them when they became Christians. When they asked the question, "What will we do with these old stories?" they answered it with three metaphors. St. Augustine says, in effect, "The classical stories and classical learning generally are useful in the way that Egyptian gold is useful. If you as a 'Hebrew' living in Egypt (i.e., traditional culture) steal the 'gold' vessels of its temple, you will be able to melt down the vessels of the Egyptians and make new vessels to use in the Lord's temple." St. Jerome used a more earthly metaphor where he spoke of the fingernails. He suggested that what you do with this captive slave girl is clean her fingernails, give her a bath and marry her. St. Augustine of England said much the same kind of thing about the pagan temples; you clean out the vital organs that are piled up in the temple, wash the blood off the walls, and make them into churches. According to this logic, Phoebus could become the "Son of Justice" which is Christ. Augustine's and Jerome's perception is largely lost to the present educational process: the perception that people who believe one set of narratives but who come to a system essentially structured around the truth of another set of narratives, come to that system with the "wrong set" of stories. One can neither wipe out the one set of narratives nor altogether destroy the system based on the other set. One can see where the two touch or clash and perform an act of translation.

Like Church fathers coming to Roman institutions, many children who come to our schools do not come with "our" set of stories "in mind." We have to help them steal our clay vessels. Education does not fill an empty vessel or inscribe upon white and beautifully unmarked tablets. Children come to us already with full vessels; we can hope that they will also find some of ours usable.

Education is a transaction in which the teacher "leads out" from the child's belief system; it is also a transaction in which the child, particularly the child who comes from a culture or neighborhood different from the teacher's, can potentially "lead" the teacher "out" from her belief system. American education has been "melting pot" education, education which sees its job as essentially one of imposing the American story on the minds of the American children, the story of Horatio Alger.[1]

Real American stories are stories cherished by many of the children who come to the schools, and there are *many* American stories: the stories of emergence of Navaho creation myths, the ghost dance and its eschatology, the myths of Dahomey and their counterparts in Caribbean and American black religion, the quiet collective stories of the Mennonite and Doukhobor. We have forgotten these stories among the eagles and the stars and the westward treks. All stories cherished, all of those stories told in the homes of kids—obscene, mythological, whatever they are—are the American story.

Children who come from outsider's cultures sometimes appropriate the school's story—the American story—in surprising ways. A first grade boy who was in one of the schools in which we are working is a member of the Omaha tribe. His parents belong to the Native American Church. The young boy was sitting on the floor one day when I came into the classroom. He had been reprimanded, mildly, by the teacher. Now he was slowly working his way back into the good graces of the teacher. He began to talk about how he and his comrades played in a field called *Pop Patch* full of broken bottles; he began to speak about how he went from Pop Patch down into a sewer, or what he called a sewer, some sort of round concrete drainage pipe in which there is water; he said that he went far, far into the sewer with his friends; then when they got far, far into the sewer, suddenly something scared them and they ran, ran, ran, and ran as fast as they could to get out. I was sitting on the floor beside him as he spoke. I said, "I know what you are talking about. I used to sometimes be in places like that, and I would be frightened and I would go running and running to get away." And he said, "Yes, bad things can happen in the dark, bad things can come. My grandmother sees these things—the men with cows' tails, she knows and sees the men with cows' tails." I said, "Does she see them in Lincoln?" and he said, "Yes. She sees them in Lincoln. They come all around Lincoln and all around the world, too. And when some of our men go far, far away to the edge, then they come and dance on the hood of the car." What he had done was to tell some of his home stories, but he had also taken one of my fears and very sensitively interpreted it for me by hypostatizing it. He had done his service from the perspective of his myth system, not from the perspective of mine.

As we were talking to one another, this very gentle talk, the regular teacher who had given the mild reprimand sat there and suddenly she was struck by the absurdity of it all—our sitting on the floor, my story, her young friend's story, our looks. Her mouth relaxed ever so gently toward a smile. The young Omaha Indian boy perceived that she was not any longer caught up in the story cycle. Immediately he began to show off by telling more and better wild, wild, stories about the men with cows' tails. His myth became an act. Mythos has become "showing off" for many Indian people and many black people, largely because of our insensitivity.

This young first grade child knows about life and death. The other day one of our people in the classroom was talking with him. He was talking about death. And then he said, "Well, Grandfather Oliver can bring the dead back to life." His Grandfather Oliver could bring the dead back to life by virtue of certain ceremonies which he did with bear rugs and other secret objects. Later he explained how he had been cured of sickness through various rites—peyote performances. What he was doing, of course, was expressing more than a superficial narrative, "a story our people tell"; he was stating his understanding of cause and effect—his scheme for apprehending the world. He was saying that if so-and-so did XYZ, then the dead would come back to life. He was saying, "If you do X, Y, and Z, then you will get over the measles and the mumps or whatever." He had himself experienced getting over the measles and the mumps by doing XYZ. The art of education does not lie in denying that sort of experience; it lies in trying to understand that experience. Once one has understood the experience, there can be some kind of transaction between the two cultures.[2]

A third example from this little boy's talk: he was talking to one of our teachers of neighborhood play having to do with cowboys and Indians. He said, "We play cowboys and Indians in our neighborhood." He was asked, "Well, what role do you play?" and he said, "Well, I like to play some kind of Indian. I play an Indian and two other boys in the neighborhood play Indian too. There are some other white boys around, and they are the cowboys." The person who was doing the interview was quite sensitive. "Well, well, I would think that three Indians could handle three cowboys any day of the week." But the Indian boy said, "No, we always lose.—We always lose." Then he added, "We play anyway, but we always lose." The boy was seeing himself as a literary figure, cast in playground play as if a character in a myth, the western stories on television which he had seen as celebration of the defeat of his own culture by the white man's. The defeat of Indian culture by white may not be what Western stories communicate to white people; to us they may say something about the relationship between "civilization" and "wilderness," between the "garden" and the place where the wild things are. In such a reading, "white" and "Indian" become metaphors. But too often for both Indian and white the vehicle in the metaphor becomes the tenor; the first grade boy, by interpreting what the western says in ways which are foreign to our preception and to the perception of most writers of westerns now but in a way which captures the racism which formerly was endemic to the westerns and the sense of defeat which his own group feels, was saying, "I am part of the system and I am not part of the system; I am part of your culture and I am not part of your culture." . . . "We always lose but we play anyway."

If a child has a sense that "we always lose but we play anyway," that will appear in his classroom action. When one speaks to this particular first grader about "doing something" in the classroom, one of his common responses will go something like this: "Well, if I did what you want me to, what I would do would be really beautiful." And you say, "Yes, it really would be beautiful." And he says, "But if it were really beautiful, the other boys would take it away from me." And you say, "No, they wouldn't take it away from you." And he says, "No, it would be really beautiful, and the other boys would take it away from me and you would let them do it to me." And then he refuses to do the beautiful thing which captured his imagination for a second. Every effort to get him to create becomes an effort to co-opt him and to produce a circumstance in which he will be humiliated by having what is beautiful and his taken from him. His response simply defines the terms according to which America's white people have dealt with America's Indians.

All school systems are mirrors of the cultural context in which they occur as are all children to a degree. Our story—the white man's story—is a competitive story. Our school story is the competitive, conqueror's story: spelldowns to get the best grades; "I see some little boys who haven't done all their arithmetic." There are many cultures and many people in America who don't believe that story, for whom that story is a destructive story.

II. **Narratives Which Classrooms Tell:** The second kind of narrative which comes into the classroom is the "competitive narrative." All of us have read it. It is expressed by the slogan which lies behind Abe Burrow's "How to Succeed in Business Without Really Trying"—that is, "How to Succeed in Business By Really Trying." Jules Henry has demonstrated the degree to which American classrooms are set up on the basis of a Horatio Alger conception of the conduct of education: "If you really try, if you work very, very hard, you will get ahead of other people; if you get ahead of the other people, I (the teacher, the infinite 'I am') will reward you." In the miniature competition among children to see who can succeed in the school business by really, really trying, the person who controls "success," who gives out the token-rewards (whether the conventional educational psychology darts or the "success experiences") is the teacher. He gives out the tokens on a fiercely competitive basis. At every level of academic understanding, at the level of affection, and at the level of managing behavior, the classroom turns into a re-writing of the Horatio Alger myth, the myth of the competitive life as the most rewarding life.

III. **Stories Kids Tell:** The third group of stories that I would like to talk about are the stories that kids tell; it is remarkable how little we know about the stories that kids tell one another. So seldom do we assume that children have a literary culture of their own. If we wish to "know children," we need also to know what they write on john walls—even if we don't believe that the words which they write are "the words of the prophet." All of the stories which they tell are important to our understanding of their narrative. I am trying to get people in my project to collect the stories which children tell and to compare these stories with their behaviors. Many have been collected and discussed by our people. Insofar as I have a sense of what they say, they say a variety of things—some of them are contradictory. They say that the world is a rather crazy place. That it is incomprehensible. Particularly is the logic of total war incomprehensible. They say that adult society is exceedingly insecure and, therefore, exceedingly square. At the same time, they say that adult society should remain as it is, but that kids should control it. Kids in elementary school and the kids who are in rebellion in college say the same kinds of things.

One of the things that made European education coherent in the Middle Ages was that the people who came to the grammar school and university educational systems had a shared narrative: the central narrative of the Christian faith which lay in the background of all of their intellectual inspiration. Children who come to school nowadays do not come to school with a shared narrative; they may in some communities. They may in Mennonite communities, they may in some American Indian communities and in a few black communities. But most kids in the modern elementary school are exceedingly isolated; they do not come with a common culture or a shared narrative. The kind of work that Geoffrey Summerfield does is partly to help kids discover some grounds of community. I guess that that is what I am trying to do.

Let me illustrate my point about the lack of shared narrative and the diversity of the stories which possess the imaginations with an incident from our practicum school. One day we brought some round tables into the classroom in the school in which we were working. We threw out the desks. We also brought some boxes into the classroom, boxes rather drab. We suggested that the children might paint the boxes. As the kids were painting along, they discovered that they could make a design eventually and the designs turned into stories or slogans. One child did a picture of the Titanic. We later discovered that that child was somehow particularly obsessed with the sinking of the Titanic. Why, I don't know. Other kids had painted "make love not war" on the surfaces of their boxes. Another child painted "SEX" in great red letters. A number of children painted "Black Power." There were billowy women paired with humped up old men made of felt. If you would match those slogans and designs with the personalities of kids, you would see a dimension of the kids' dream world which would never have appeared in the classroom up to that point. As I watched them paint designs on the boxes, it occurred to me that these kids had a buried life which I had not perceived! This life was not coming out in the classroom. These were exceedingly hostile children. When we disciplined them, they were angry, and when they were allowed freedom, they had a sort of classroom riot.

Later we came to the notion that maybe the children could

act out some of the things that they seemed to be saying on these boxes. Perhaps they could act out their private fantasies. They did a bit of play acting. Then they attempted to construct a kind of collective fantasy—an artificial shared narrative. And so it was that we encouraged certain kinds of acting-out behavior in the classroom.

Here one could see what black power and sex and the sinking of the Titanic meant. At the beginning of the sequence, we asked the kids to look in the mirror. We thought that we would get some remarks about identity from our acting with the kids, from having them pour over a mirror like Narcissus. We got nothing about identity. In fact we found that the children generally didn't say much about who they were unless they were on very relaxed terms with adults and felt very trusting of them. It almost seemed at first as though some of these young men and women didn't have anything to say about themselves. But that was our ignorance and *their* timidity and not *their* deficiency. When we got over to the mirror, the children said nothing about their own sense of *who they were,* who it was that was appearing there. What they did say was much about *what they wanted.* And what they wanted were their friends, their mothers, affection, and affectionate talk.

We went next to the mythic sequence. It was clear to us from our study of the children's fantasies that they would respond to an earth mother type. This figure we called "Mother Earth"; the children were willing to interact with her in various sorts of ways. Why? Perhaps because almost all of these children came from homes where there were no fathers; as soon as I came in to the play as a masculine figure I was cast in the role of a demon-wizard. The children forced that role upon me. Thus, the kids in their freely improvised setting were telling something about the mythos of the masculine and feminine in their world. The boys in the group cast themselves as my fellow demons. The boys were already identifying themselves as outsiders; the girls were identifying themselves as squares. The boys figured themselves as no good. The girls thought of themselves as having to move towards some type of responsibility. The girls teased the heck out of the boys from the position of authority; hence, the boys were constantly in a position of sort of a Miltonic Satan being mad at a female God. As the improvised dramatic sequence moved along, the black children tended to place themselves on the side of the forces of evil. The white children and the girls tended to place themselves on the side of the forces of good. For instance, when the children of Mother Earth came to the earth and found a black child sitting in the room, they said concerning him "that he shoots people, that he is cruel, that he does cruel things, etc." One black child said, "He should live," and some white child said, "No, he should die." Someone said, "What does he do that is evil?" The "good children" said, "He hits people. He runs them down and he says bad things about them." They conducted a mock trial which "proved" that he was one with the forces of evil. They went on to attack the teacher. The teacher became the enemy: "You are the evilest one in this place; you scold people, you make us work as if we were slaves." A black child spoke, and in her remarks, a long history of authority systems came out: "She scolds people, she makes us work as if we were slaves." "Only evil with black on have to work. Only the ones with black on have to work. Do white blouses have to work?" Black people are the people who have to work.

Some kids began to say, "We want war." They wanted to make war and some other kids began to chant with them. And when the kids were on the side of the wizard evil they began to oppose the people who were standing with Mother Earth and saying that there should be peace, that it is no good to fight. They said, "My people, my people will tell you what is good; that is to fight a war and to kill the people. To burn their houses, cook them in the ovens, to grind them up." The girls allied to Mother Earth responded to this: "There shouldn't be any such thing as war. You are at war. You are the crazy one who works at killing people. We are for peace and order." The evil people responded: "We are strong men. We are strong." Then eventually one of the kids who was on the side of Mother Earth said, "Peace is power." Up to this time the drama had supposed that Mother Earth and her pacific forces were weak; the gestalt of the story was broken with the remark: "Peace is power." Suddenly the whole group went to pieces. They didn't know how to respond. The dramatic play came apart. The forces of evil began a sort of war dance to burn up the forces of good. Later the forces of creation and life began to reconstruct the natural world again. They constructed it pretty largely as a pastoral world. They gradually began to elaborate cities and industries and so forth. The interesting thing here was that most of the discussion concerned whether there should be families in this world, whether there should be parents. Ultimately the kids opted for parents, and they opted for parents of a very secure square sort.

What I am trying to illustrate for you is the mythos that lies behind the surface of the narrative composed in a spontaneous drama by these children. In some ways, what they said reflects attitudes common in western civilization. There are the struggles between the forces of light and the forces of darkness. There is the picture of a pastoral innocence which prevailed at the beginning. The kids' dreams are, in broad outline, part of the dreams of all men in western civilization.

The children begin with the cosmic warfare in the forces of light and the forces of darkness; when they began a new creation, they began a kind of Eden-like world. But it is interesting that in this dramatic scene evil was a positive force. It was not simply a deprivation of good as it is traditionally seen to be in the western world; evil and darkness were at least as strong as the forces of light. The choice between evil and good was not really a choice between these but a choice between two alternatively strong forces. The discussion of parents suggests that these children do not really like the struggle between generations. They want to be square. They want to be members of a very square middle-class "responsible" home. The kids are being influenced by the Eden story, but they are also influenced by their lives. Many of these kids began their lives on a farm—the black kids in Mississippi and Alabama and the white kids in Nebraska and Iowa. Our ghettos are full of children who come from families dispossessed by technology, whose first and fondest memories are memories of play in the rural areas, and who have come to an urban civilization which they can't understand and where they are hopelessly lost.

This free dramatic activity and a great many other similar activities can be useful in that they help us to understand the belief systems of kids. They can also be useful to kids, helping them to construct as it were a common myth and mythos. We ought to use whatever devices we can to help kids to construct a story held in common for themselves.

IV. **Mythology:** The fourth kind of story that I want to talk about is the myth in the conventional sense—received story which is part of the belief system of other cultures. It is tremendously important that children study who their people have been, what the basic belief systems, of which they inherit only the withered stumps, were. They should understand who they were, and they should know who other people were and are. They can do this by studying myth which comes from Western culture or other cultures. Most of what we learn in such study has to do with other people, but some of what we learn has to do with what *our* homes, schools and children are. One day I was traveling from Kansas to Nebraska in my car. The children were misbehaving, and I didn't have any book with me to read to the children so I read what I had. The only thing I had with me was a copy of *Hesiod*. I was trying to get up material which I could present to an undergraduate class in "Classical Roots of English Literature." My son was about four years old at that time, and he was misbehaving. I was too tired to make up a story to tell him. So I decided that I would read him a story. I opened *Hesiod.* The vocabulary of the theogony is exceedingly difficult. I couldn't read it to him in my adult vocabulary. But I read it substituting words as he needed for understanding. The story that I chose to read happened to be the story which tells how the gods and the Titans fought each other. When my son heard the story he was tremendously excited. By the time the story was over we had reached home, and so we went in and he got out a paint box and he painted a tremendous picture. In the picture was an enormous red figure with rocks in its hands, a beautiful, tremendous thing looking like Captain Marvel or embodied electric energy. In the forefront of the picture was a little ugly blue figure with hundreds of arms around the edge, and I asked Andrew who the large red figure was and he said, "The large red figure is a Titan." The little blue figure was a hundred arms. There was no Zeus in the painting. It was perfectly obvious where Andrew's loyalties lay; his loyalties were with the Titans and not with the Hundred Arms or with Zeus.

I don't know exactly what my son's picture meant; I would suppose that, by leaving out Zeus and allying himself with the Titan, he was saying something about the authority over him, about his father and about his having cried in the car and what it all meant.

To me the story was another story. It was a story partly of what Greece was and of what Zeus meant to it as "wisdom" set over against brute strength. It was to me, a person who is born to a traditional Christian home, a story which recalls the scene in *Paradise Lost* where Milton deliberately adopts the Hesiodic mode and creates a battle in which Christ plays the role of Zeus, the archangels playing the role of the Hundred Arms and Satan the role of the Titan.

In that hour of reading and painting, there came to me my son's perception of what I was, my perception of who my son was, and yet another perception: where we had all been as a people. *Hesiod* had told me something about the belief-system by which I have lived, about that by which my child lives, and about my home. He could also tell us about schools.

---

1. *A Pride of Lions* (Lincoln, Nebraska: Nebraska Curriculum Development Center: NCDE).

2. Claude Levi-Strauss, *The Savage Mind* (Chicago: University of Chicago Press, 1966).

# Current Theories and Practices

# Part Three

*Speak to children and read to them—often. They need to hear frequently the tunes of our language so that when they encounter them in reading the refrains will be familiar.*

# The World of Children's Books and Reading

## by William A. Jenkins

The children's book world could probably more aptly be called a universe with planets and satellites and constellations, in this case visible to the naked eye for all who would gaze at them. There are stars of the first magnitude and, unfortunately, books that, though they bear the label "for children," are as inconsequential as cosmic dust.

Covering this entire field in one brief discussion is almost like trying to scan the entire sky to view in one evening all the stars and planets. It simply can't be done. I shall, therefore, attempt to resolve the dilemma posed by my title by pointing to a few of the major bodies in this constellation, both stars and planets. Some will be presented to you in the form of biases; others, as random thoughts which I consider important.

Dr. William A. Jenkins
Dean
School of Education
Portland State University

### The World of Children's Books

My first bias is that children's books are for real. That is, children's books are part of all literature—British, American, Russian, Scandinavian, white, black, yellow, old, new. They belong in the mainstream. They are not back-water, minor branch, or dry stream bed. In all categories they are very much the same as adult books, except that perhaps children have picture books, and adults rarely do. With this similarity, then, the treatment should be much the same with the emphasis on the same product, reading. This thought leads me to my second bias.

Children's books are primarily to be read—for enjoyment, for knowledge, for answers, and for self-imposed whiling-away-hours. This means that considerations of dissection, didacticism, and other-directed diversion are secondary, if not totally inappropriate. To cut off a two-inch square of a painting for analysis is to violate a painter's artistic creative entity. The same is true of the dissection of literary works for children. It calls for literary anti-vivisection laws. Only in rare and completely defensible instances should such biopsies take place. For example, reading so that book reports can be written is a bit like saying that you eat just to get rid of some of the food in the world. Hundreds of teachers, unfortunately, still see reading primarily as a means to the book report end. Reading literature for social studies ends is equally as indefensible. It is like threshing wheat so that one may have chaff. True, there are chaff-lovers in the world, but there is also a Flat World Society and both groups are more than a bit ludicrous.

My third bias has to do with indispensable books. I frankly doubt if there are any books that a child *should* read. I dare say that this habit was created out of considerations of teacher convenience and, like so many habits, eventually was considered Divine Truth.

There are just too many fine books that most children should have the opportunity to enjoy, to restrict them to just a few. As we introduce youngsters to choice books, we should at the same time encourage them to reject them. We want always to respect the child's right to his own taste. However, taste for good literature is not inherent in childhood. No child is born with a knowledge and love of good books; he develops this as his parents and teachers read to him when he is very young, and later as he himself is able to read and appreciate good literature.

Not many years ago the avid reader could read most of the books which were published, the good and the bad. Each year thousands of books for juveniles are published. No child could read them all nor would we want him to do so. Many of these books are of mediocre quality. Some are poor indeed. Today, with so many titles from which to choose, it is possible for a child to read many books, and yet not read an outstanding one. He needs guidance from the librarian, his teachers, and his parents.

Still another of my biases on children's books is that teachers should not be satisfied with letting a child read a mediocre book. There are few dangers in reading mediocre books, but they rob the child of time he might have spent in reading better ones. Time is an important consideration in children's reading, because the years of childhood are limited. They in turn limit the number of children's books an individual youngster will read as well as the period of his life during which he will be interested in children's books.

## The World of Reading

In the world of reading as opposed to the world of books, I also have some biases. The first has to do with wide reading. Wide reading, free reading, coupled with the teacher's and librarian's enthusiasm, can lead to greater competence than any specific reading approach. This notion is supported in the experience of hundreds of teachers, and in the professional literature. For example, when children are not given freedom to read, their reading becomes an exercise in defiance. The concern that they read *only* the best may be unfounded, though logical. Children who read comics—the source of worry for many a teacher or parent—also read a variety of other things. For this reason an important step in development must be simply to develop the reading habit, the public library habit, the reading-for-fun habit.

The business of giving freedom of selection has been tried by many teachers, with satisfying results. For instance, in a school in Long Island each grade made a list of the new books which class members wanted the school to include in its biannual order. The students used *The Horn Book Magazine,* the New York *Herald Tribune,* the *Wilson Bulletin,* and so forth—a worthwhile activity in itself. The arrival of the new books was eagerly anticipated, and once on hand they were read with the greatest of zest. Needless to say, the lists were as good, if not better, than those the teachers and librarians had assembled in the past.

The second point on reading relates to expected behavior. I think we have often been off base here. Philip Jackson of the University of Chicago has pointed out that man does many things in solitude, including reading. Jackson's analysis of reading shows it to be not only solitary, but also personal, private, and individual.[1] When we have children read in school, the first thing we do is socialize the activity. We destroy this thing which is in large part imagination, in the way that fantasy play of children is destroyed when an adult breaks in. By so doing we can inhibit the unique meaning which the reader may obtain. We invade his privacy. We prevent the physical reaction which the solitary reader who does not know he is being observed has: yawning, stretching, chuckling, guffawing, weeping, squirming, scratching, and so on. We require social rather than private behavior. By so doing we can make the reader uneasy.

In socializing reading we organize it, give it purpose, and set it in a competitive environment. We emphasize speed, though most other aspects of living are permitted to occur at a natural pace.

Jackson's study is fascinating and, while one can gainsay each of his findings and arguments, the study has important implications for teaching reading. Since reading is individual, perhaps there should be more time for the student to pick what suits his fancy. Since reading is private, we should not socialize all of our reading-literature activities. Perhaps rooms for private reading—like faculty carrels in the library, or booths in a language laboratory—should be provided. At any rate, Jackson recommends that perhaps we should permit the stretching, yawning, squirming, disarray and disorder that the reader displays in his progress through the mind and imagination of another as he reads the other's words.

### Apogees and Perigees of Reading

Another bias is related to the current controversy over the approaches to teaching reading. I think it has taken too much of our time and energy. I'd like to offer a completely abandoned, somewhat indefensible answer to the question "What really works in teaching reading?" by saying that *everything* works.

Specifically, I think learning to read by using good literature works. To be literature a selection must meet several criteria. Suffice it here to say that written selections which make a difference in the child—how he feels, how he sees things, how he thinks about himself and other human beings—work in teaching reading. Personal reading which touches kids *where they are* works.

Critical reading, reading which invites, encourages, and even involuntarily elicits a reaction works. In a depth definition of reading, it is a cognitive process with thought preceding, during and after the reading act. Thinking and reading cannot, should not, be separated.

Tie reading to talking. It works. A writer must "speak" to a child as a child speaks to others. One theory says writing is talk written down. Not quite. But the commonalities must be capitalized on in teaching reading. The capital will bear interest.

Speak to children and read to them—often. They need to hear frequently the tunes of our language so that when they encounter them in reading the refrains will be familiar.

The eclectic approaches of today's better basal readers are effective in teaching reading. The better basals advocate a mix of phonics and recognition reading; a mix of the code emphasis (ITA, linguistics, and phonics) and the meaning emphasis. In this regard, we might ask in passing if learning to read by sight recognition is not also learning to decode? At any rate, they advocate the use of many trade books, not just the basals themselves. More importantly, the better basals advocate the widest possible range of language activities when one is teaching reading to capitalize on the interrelatedness of all of the language arts.

So you see, practically anything *can* work in teaching reading. Whether it *will* depends on the teacher—on his knowledge of children, of books, of reading approaches; on his enthusiasm and his love of learner and learning.

Let me now turn to a specific type of reading matter and a specific type of reading, poetry. As would be true of a discussion of any type of reading and any type of reading matter, I cannot discuss poetry apart from a discussion of children, too.

## Children and Poetry, Stellar Dimensions

John Ciardi defines intelligence as the ability to see essential likenesses and essential differences when you compare things.[2] A higher form of intelligence is the ability to see likenesses and differences within likenesses. And a still higher form of intelligence is the ability to see some of the differences within the likenesses and some of the likenesses within the differences. This is, in part, what education is all about, and that, in part, is what the poet does.

Ciardi also says that the difference between a savage and a civilized person is that the savage simply has not received enough news from mankind. If we extend this metaphor, a library is a news center; a book is a news medium; and a poet is a special kind of reporter or commentator. This is one big reason children should get to know poets and poetry—for the news they get about mankind and the differences and likenesses they will find in the poetry they read. More reasons in a moment.

Our American attitude toward poetry is not shared by the entire world. Paul Hazard points out that in France poetry is not viewed as a luxury to be dealt with before a certain age. Rather, poetry is viewed as a rational pleasure that must be clearly understood. The idea of fascination where there is nothing to understand, just fantasy, resonance and rhyme, seems lunacy to the French.

In this country we have the very strong belief that poetry for young children must be nonsensical. Perhaps this is right, but too often we do not get beyond the nonsense poetry. And there appears to be a gap between what we give children in the early grades and what they read later on in high school. In the middle and upper grades poetry is neglected altogether, because in these grades we seldom read to children. I think that poetry is of the essence of life and therefore it should be both of laughter and tears and of joy and sorrow. Helen Parkhurst has tried to explain it this way: "The difference between prose and poetry is the difference between the speaking voice and the singing. Two things qualitatively distinct, and yet incapable of exact description, but though distinct they comprehend a wide range of gradations that intervene between them." [3] The crux of the matter is that we sometimes forget that poetry, the language of singing, is not only used to sing happily, but also to sing sadly. Voltaire said poetry is the music of the soul, but above all, of great and feeling souls.

What I am saying to you is that to let children see that poetry contains the essence of life, one must go beyond nonsense and euphonious eruptions. The dividends received later when the students are in high school and college will prove this investment shrewd and calculated.

## An Atlas of Poetry

In some of his best poetry for children, John Ciardi has the ability to use the language of childhood so effectively that the child addressed easily sees the humor of his situation and comes away from the encounter with a smile.

> Someone's face was all frowned shut,
>     All squeezed full of grims and crinkles,
> Pouts and scowls and gloomers, but
>     I could see behind the wrinkles—
>
> Even with her face a-twist,
>     I saw Someone peeking through.
> And when Someone's nose was kissed
>     Guess who came out giggling? YOU! [4]

My thoughts on children and poetry stem from an interest in humanity, viewed through the eyes of the poet; news from humanity interpreted by the poet. What more can we do for children in our classes than to teach them to feel, to see, all of humanity—to laugh with their fellow man, and at themselves?

I think we can teach them about the news medium, poetry, itself. What better way than through a poem, "Unfolding Bud" by Naoshi Koriyama:

One is amazed
By a water-lily bud
Unfolding
With each passing day,
Taking on a richer color
And new dimensions.

One is not amazed,
At a first glance,
By a poem,
Which is as tight-closed
As a tiny bud

Yet one is surprised
To see the poem
Gradually unfolding,
Revealing its rich inner self,
As one reads it
Again
And over again.[5]

Teach them also to read news pictures as in "Child on Top of a Greenhouse" by Theodore Roethke:

The wind billowing out the seat of my britches,
My feet crackling splinters of glass and dried putty,
The half-grown chrysanthemums staring up like accusers,
Up through the streaked glass, flashing with sunlight,
A few white clouds all rushing eastward,
A line of elms plunging and tossing like horses,
And everyone, everyone pointing up and shouting! [6]

Show them the cryptic language, meaningless as individual words, but powerful as a complete artistic entity, as in "Elegy for Jog" by John Ciardi:

Stiff-dog death, all froth on a bloody chin,
sniffs at the curb. Skinny-man death, his master,
opens the traffic's hedge to let him in.
Jog was his name, silliness his disaster.

He wasn't satisfied to scare the truck:
he had to bite the tire. Fools have no luck.[7]

And show them the power of words to move mountains, give
man a soul, and awaken long dormant aspirations, as in Langston Hughes' editorial called "Dreams":

Hold fast to dreams
For if dreams die
Life is a broken-winged bird
That cannot fly.

Hold fast to dreams
For when dreams go
Life is a barren field
Frozen with snow.[8]

Give children news reports from other times and places such
as that contained in Stevenson's "The Lamplighter":

For we are very lucky with a lamp before the door,
And Leerie stops to light it as he lights so many more.
And O! before you hurry by with ladder and with light,
O Leerie, see a little child and nod to him tonight.[9]

Even of the creation of the world, by James Weldon Johnson:

And God stepped out on space,
And he looked around and said,
"I'm lonely—
I'll make me a world." [10]

And then just to round things out, bring them back to local
news, the reports of everyday experiences, such as Mary Neville's
"Complaining Day":

I was complaining
Today
I thought of all the
Bad Things:

Make my bed.
Carry out garbage
Go to bed earlier than
Other kids.
Can't watch T.V. on
School nights.

But I remember some
Good Things:

    Woody,
    Mother and Dad,
    Not sick much,
    Not dead,
    My bike,
    Saturday.

    That is quite a
    Lot
    Of good ones.[11]

Finally, but by no means least of all, as we work with children there may be occasion and need for an antidote for pomposity, a cure for self-gyrating egos, a palliative for aggression. There are poetic news reports for this purpose, too. This one, and the commentator is anonymous, is called "The Water Cure."

    Sometimes when you're feeling important
    Sometimes when your ego's in bloom
    Sometimes when you take it for granted
    You're the best qualified in the room.
    Sometimes when you feel your going
    Would leave an unfillable hole,
    Just follow this simple instruction
    And see how it humbles your soul.

    Take a bucket and fill it with water
    Put your hand in—up to your wrist.
    Take it out—and the hole that's remaining
    Is a measure of how you'll be missed.
    You can splash all you please as you enter,
    You can stir up the water galore,
    But STOP—and you'll find in a minute
    That it looks quite the same as before.
    There's a moral in this quaint expression—
    Just do the best that you can;
    Be proud of yourself, but remember,
    There is no indispensable man.

## Some Random Interstellar Excursions on Reading

What constitutes a good reading program? Each of us has his own answer. Let me, therefore, attempt to mention some things which frequently are overlooked.

Skill in reading for information in the various content areas is needed. Time must be provided for recreational or pleasure reading. Children should be read to, as well. Some corrective work is needed. These four categories are not mutually exclusive. Basal reading may well be reading in social studies or science content. Reading in science may be informational as well as pleasurable. Skills in comprehension and interpretation apply to books read for pleasure as well as books read for information. Corrective measures can apply to any category in reading in which children have not developed skills equal to their ability.

Despite the fact that the four categories of reading overlap and different authors assign different names to them, it is necessary to consider the categories in order to make clear the constituents of a good reading program. Reading is not confined to a basal reading series. In fact, because it has been misinterpreted in the past, questions are currently raised as to whether a basal reading program is needed at all for teaching the basic skills or whether other materials or individualized reading provide a better basis for skill building. I believe that *initial* teaching of a skill is best done with a group using a common material, and *continued use* and *development* of that skill is best carried on in a variety of functional applications, using many books and materials. Except for the very early grades, good basal reading series often contain folk tales, poetry, social studies and science material, comics, recipes, etc., in addition to the simple stories for which they are so often credited, or rather discredited.

There are three major areas of skill development: mechanics of word analysis, understanding and critical reaction to what is read, and reference skills. Turning to the first, even the bright children have not necessarily developed the mechanics of word analysis as well as they might. We know that remedial reading clinics are partly tenanted with such children. This is true in some measure because bright children often dislike drill and are impatient with details, so if reading does not come to them with ease right at the start, they begin to dislike and avoid reading and then fall behind. Often we don't even realize that such children are in difficulty with reading because they do listen and pick up many of the answers without reading. Also, they often grade higher than their functional reading level on standardized tests because they are able to piece together the bits of what they *can* read well enough to select the correct answers from the multiple choices. Informal reading inventories may find out how well the child actually reads connected materials. Otherwise, his reading difficulties may remain unknown.

Bright children seem to prefer the opportunity of discovering the underlying principles of phonetic and structural analysis through *analysis of words that represent those principles* rather than being told the principle and then being required to drill.

Depending on grade level, and the difficulty of the selection, good writing can be appreciated for its beauty, the mood conveyed, the characters described, the style, etc. Figurative speech can be identified; symbolism can be responded to; colloquialisms can be enjoyed. Reading *aloud* to a group and then thinking aloud with them about specific parts of the selection may be one of the best ways to help children learn to be analytical in their own reading. It may also help build their own skills of oral and written expression.

Becoming analytic about words, then, is not confined to word recognition skills but it can also be applied to developing a second and perhaps more important basic skill, which concerns itself with meaning and interpretation.

The problem of getting children under way in learning to read continues to vex us. There is no easy position, but there is a great variety of possibilities in getting them under way. Children from unusual backgrounds or those who are extremely gifted can learn to read without extensive or intensive guidance. But it would seem to me that normal children can obtain a great deal of value from reading a carefully developed basal reading series, when the teacher fits the approaches in such a series to each child's needs, interests, and abilities. The advantage, of course, of a basal series, when accompanied by workbooks and teacher's manuals, is that the thinking of a great number of individuals has gone into the preparation of these materials, and the ideas contained therein, at least theoretically, will be superior to the ideas and approaches from a single individual. For beginning teachers, of course, such a series is a must because it provides them with the security and the knowledge to do a good job. Few teachers, moreover, have the knowledge of vocabulary control which limits the number of concepts and ideas with which a child must wrestle. When a teacher feels that interest and motivation are not fostered by a basal series she, of course, can use a supplementary basal series, or turn to trade books. The task of developing the requisite number of skills, the proper attitude, and the optimum understanding need not be viewed as antithetical to enjoying reading. Rather the two ends of the pole must be brought together so that reading can become an activity to be sought and used with satisfaction.

## Aquarius: Basal Readers

It is a fact that basal readers are changing. In an article which appeared in *Educational Leadership* not long ago, Dr. Charlotte Huck pointed to these changes:

1) Vocabulary controls are lifted or eased at a considerably earlier level than heretofore. Unnatural or stilted sentence patterns are avoided.

2) The content of the readers is changing dramatically. They now include every genre of literature, articles, newspaper accounts and features, and improved illustrations by a variety of illustrators. They are attempting to be normal reading, and to approach the quality of good literature.

3) Readers have become multi-ethnic in character—Negroes, Chinese, Mexicans, and Italians people these books. The unreal Caucasian world of yesteryear's books has disappeared, in part, in the readers of at least five publishing companies, but with varying degrees of success.[12]

One basic position says that the preparatory phase for reading instruction is principally to develop in the child a desire to read and to create or foster his readiness to read. More vital, though, is the position that the urge to read comes out of talking and listening; from observing; by being read to; and through experiences. It has been shown through various studies that when a child does not talk, or is not talked to by adults in his formative stages, his interest and concern for language is very minimal. Where he does not have experiences, he has little basis for language work. If he is not read to at home, his interest in learning to read is thereby decreased, and if through his relationships with other human beings he has not developed the skill or the desire to observe, again his interest in learning to read is decreased. One of the major tasks of teachers, therefore, is to fill the gap which may have been created by the omission of any of these background experiences. Tinker and McCullough, among others, have found that perhaps twenty-five percent of the children who enter first grade are not ready to learn to read because of the deficiency of one or more of these important experiential facets.

### Star Clusters: Organizing for Reading

The question of which type of organization for instruction should be used during the teaching of reading is one that has no answer, and many answers. The undifferentiated or whole class approach, the group approach, or the individualized approach all have their advocates, and each has its merits. Perhaps the question should not be which of these approaches should be used but rather which approach should be used when. Whenever a problem, a topic, or a question is of importance to the entire group, the entire group should be instructed at one time. Basic information about books, a lesson, a unit, a film, an activity, an experience, calls for whole class instruction. Choral reading by student groups, or oral reading by a librarian, teacher, or gifted reader, should be presented to the entire group. One of the values of whole class instruction is the sense of belonging to the class which it provides for every child.

Probably the most sensible approach is to use the individualized program when it best fits the needs of the readers. This means that some basic lessons should be taught in the whole class while other skills are taught in small groups. At the same time the individualized program meets individual purposes and interests and the demands of certain work type and recreational classroom objectives. It very definitely is true that one of the problems with the individualized approach is finding a sufficient number of books for individualized programs. In those schools where the commitment is great to a basal series without trade books to provide supplementary instructional materials, the approach is hurt by the lack of a sufficient number of books. Books and more books of many types and levels are necessary to meet the varying interests and recreational and study needs of children within a class. Where the school library is not adequate, a teacher should attempt to build a class library by gathering books which are suitable from whatever source that may be available. They may be chosen using guides such as *Adventuring with Books* and *The Children's Catalogue*, published by the National Council of Teachers of English.

The individualized approach is basically self-teaching in that a child will guide himself in reading which is necessary and beneficial to him.

Reading can be the means of integrating various language arts processes, emphasizing their cognitive, thoughtful aspects. Because of its focus on comprehension, evaluation, organization, and retention, objectives which are valid for all of the language arts, it may serve this purpose very well. Reading is the point at which vocabulary can be related to experience. Along with writing it can help one understand ideas, concepts, processes; recognize relationships; make comparisons; draw inferences; and reflect and interpret. It is the integrating point for dictionary, encyclopedia, bibliography, and library study. It is a source for teaching critical evaluation of ideas and materials, the extracting of essentials from non-essentials. Similarly, along with writing it helps one to learn to organize ideas and show relationships and to develop retentive powers.

**Luminosity: The Matter of Values**

Matthew Arnold said that conduct is three-fourths of life. If one assumes that reading and books can make a difference, that they can affect conduct and character, they then become essential ingredients in life. But let us emphasize that the reading of literature is complete only when the reader himself goes on to consider that it can or may make a difference in him. John Ciardi says that a book can make a reader "quietly passionate" about an idea, an event, or a person.

Enjoyment, like beauty, may be its own excuse for being. We, therefore, do not have to defend the pleasure that one can find in reading; as teachers we should expect and insist that it occur. However, enjoyment is not an automatic outcome. Nor will it occur from the same reading experience for all children and youth. They respond to reading according to their experiences, personalities, and preoccupations. Their interpretations differ just as their tastes do. And we should not forget that one interpretation may be as true or honest as another. Most of all, we must remind ourselves that their pleasures may not be our pleasures, nor the same as those of other class members.

### Comets: Transitory and Temporal

Regarding contemporary books, books that deal with current social problems, again there are many views. I offer you *one* position.

Lionel Trilling recently pointed out that the notable books of an age in part have to be determined by "a culture's hum and buzz of implication." That which is read and that which is important to read are related to the conscience and determination of a people. The proletarian novels of the twenties and thirties, as examples, were an important genre for those times, even though we now view them as dysfunctional museum pieces. Just so, literature which is critically needed in the school today well may become tomorrow's relics. But it will have served, just as we must.

Even so—to stick with my focus on literature—our dilemma is partly solved if we remember that literature has no life of its own. It is a parasite which comes to life and is nourished only within us. It must emphasize humanity yesterday, forever, but especially *now*. Literature earns its way by being related to life. And, as James E. Miller, Jr., Owen Thomas, and Robert C. Pooley, among others, have pointed out—even though literature is a primary means for man to bring order and control to his life, it in turn is ordered and controlled by life.

### Again, the Universe

My view of the children's world of books and reading is that it presents open possibilities. Its greatest measure of value is its ability to touch and to arouse. The teacher points to facets of books, of stories, of poems, and leads children into the works. She does not attempt to create satisfactions and appreciations. These forever reside in the reader himself. Neither putting them in nor taking them out for examination, evaluation, or improvement is proper teacher behavior.

One final thought: many of us know that the child from grade three or four to grade eight comes back to school in September and is told to write about his vacation. He's up to his gills with this banal and thoughtless assignment. In the same fashion, repetition can occur with books. *Mr. Popper's Penguins* in second grade, in third grade and maybe again in fourth grade may be a bit too much. It may have been too much the first time. And are discoveries of haiku really discoveries? The children may have already discovered it, and had it.

Our world is moving rapidly on and changing and so are both the children and the books in that world. But books can still capture for them the pleasure and joys of the moment, the problems and prizes of the past. We cannot measure—though we know that it is there—the lasting effects that the world of books will have on the children of our world. But if we can make the moments of encounter—the space shots—rich with experiences, golden with joy, and at some time touch each child where he is at, no matter where, as Northrop Frye puts it, we have helped him "possess" literary art. I think "possession" is what matters, in his world and in ours.

1. Philip Jackson, *Meeting Individual Differences in Reading,* edited by H. Alan Robinson (Chicago: University of Chicago Press, 1964).

2. John Ciardi, "Why Teach Poetry?" *Virginia Journal of Education* (December 1960), pp. 17-18.

3. Helen Parkhurst, *Beauty: An Interpretation of Art and the Imaginative Life* (New York: Harcourt Brace Jovanovich, Inc., 1930), pp. 205-206.

4. John Ciardi, "Someone," in *Birthday Candles Burning Bright: A Treasury of Birthday Poetry,* edited by Sara and John Brewton (New York: The Macmillan Company, 1960). Reprinted by permission of the author.

5. Naoshi Koriyama, "Unfolding Bud," in *The Christian Science Monitor* (July 13, 1957), Home Forum page. Reprinted by permission from *The Christian Science Monitor* © 1957, The Christian Science Publishing Society. All rights reserved.

6. "Child on Top of a Greenhouse," by Theodore Roethke. Copyright 1946, Editorial Publications, Inc. From the book *Collected Poems of Theodore Roethke* by Theodore Roethke. Reprinted by permission of Doubleday & Company, Inc.

7. John Ciardi, "Elegy for Jog," in *As If, Poems New and Selected* by John Ciardi (New Brunswick, New Jersey: Rutgers University Press, 1955). Reprinted by permission of the author.

8. Langston Hughes, "Dreams," from *The Dream Keeper and Other*

*Poems* by Langston Hughes (New York: Alfred A. Knopf, Inc., 1932, 1966). Reprinted by permission of the publisher.

9. Robert Louis Stevenson, "The Lamplighter," from *A Child's Garden of Verses* by Robert Louis Stevenson (New York: Charles Scribner's Sons, 1895).

10. James Weldon Johnson, "Creation," from *God's Trombones* by James Weldon Johnson (New York: The Viking Press, Inc., 1927). Reprinted by permission of the publisher.

11. Mary Neville, "Complaining Day," from *Woody and Me* by Mary Neville (New York: Pantheon Books, a Division of Random House, Inc., 1966). Reprinted by permission of the publisher.

12. Charlotte Huck, "The Changing Character of Basic Reading Materials," *Educational Leadership* Vol. 22 (No. 6) (March 1965), pp. 377-381, 439.

*The confluence of the new insights from linguistics and from the psychology of verbal behavior supported by the awesome data-gathering powers of the computer will not only delineate sharply the essential skills but demonstrate how to plan different kinds of strategies, tactics, and pacings for different kinds of children.*

# Trends in Reading: Elementary and Secondary

## by William J. Iverson

The rate of change in elementary reading instruction has sharply accelerated during the last decade. In the first place, we have clarified our view of the reading process. In the sixties, linguistics made a marked impact on reading instruction. If you look at the review of research in reading, *Handbook of Research on Teaching*,[1] published by the American Educational Research Association in 1963, you will find almost no mention of the uses of linguistic scholarship in reading instruction. Now its effects on concepts of reading instruction are everywhere. In addition, thanks largely to federal funding, we are now getting higher quality input from psychological research. Furthermore, the rising concern for culturally different children has brought new interest from the sociologists and the anthropologists. And

Dr. William J. Iverson
Professor, Department of Education
Stanford University

the various Project English curricula have altered the content through which the reading process is currently being developed.

Now what kinds of changes have these new views of reading brought to elementary reading instruction? They can be discussed in four categories:

1. Changes in concepts of readiness.
2. Changes in materials and methods of instruction.
3. Changes in organization for instruction.
4. Changes in means of evaluation.

First, changes in concepts of readiness. I believe that we need a high degree of focus to add strength directly to what the child must do in order to read. This focus should be on linguistic, visual, and intellectual factors. But the testing instruments which might diagnose the component elements of these three factors leave something to be desired. Are the intelligence tests really culture-free? Or is there some way we could differentiate between what is native competence and what is cultural competence? Then, there is the readiness test itself. We still lack effective diagnostic guides to visual perception skills or to linguistic skills which readiness tests ought to provide. We need the kind of readiness instrument which singles out the component elements of these visual and linguistic skills. The present tests simply do not give us the kind of guidance which tells us what is present and what is lacking, nor do they suggest what to do about it. Robert Calfee in his work at Wisconsin makes it clear that evidence of the validity of readiness tests as diagnostic indicators is lacking. Nor does it seem to him that directions for furthering readiness are apparent. In short, Calfee is convinced that readiness tests do not provide well-defined measures of the component skills related to reading performance.[2] That judgment of Calfee suggests that we need to be cautious about delaying reading instruction purely on the basis of present readiness test results. Instead, until better instruments are available, we might find in teacher judgment and in the initial teaching of reading itself the best present means of defining what a child needs to get ready to read.

Now let me turn to changes in materials and methods of instruction. The predominant medium for instruction remains the basic reader. But it too has changed, changed in vocabulary, controls, content, and pacing. Vocabulary control now ends in some cases with the second-grade reader and in almost all cases with the third-grade book. The skills in word-analysis and identification associated with this vocabulary control, principally context, phonics, and structural analysis, are also completely introduced in most series by the end of the second or third-grade level. Formerly, the word attack skills were spaced out until the end of the sixth grade. Beyond vocabulary, changes in sentence style have also come to the basic reader. There is less "See, seraphim, see" than there used to be. But systematic instruction in syntax and in intonation is yet to come. Indeed, optimum sequencing in any of the linguistic elements (phonology, morphology, syntax, or intonation) is still to be discovered.

Content, in the basic reader, has also been modified. Especially in the middle grades there is a wider variety of materials. The basic reader is still dominated by story-type material. Systematic use of exposition is still lacking. But at least, an attempt has been made in story to secure greater representation of America's cultural diversity. There are black and brown children now in the stories. There is more story situated in the city and less out in the country. Illustrations also reflect this wider view of life in the sixties.

Pacing changes are reflected in the basic readers through providing more than one level of instruction per grade. There still is predominantly one reader at a grade level. But at least one publisher now issues three readers per grade: one at grade level, one below grade level, one above. I look for this trend to grow.

Independent of the basic reader are hosts of special charts, books, booklets, and workbooks, all focusing largely on word identification. Kenneth Goodman of Wayne State University is right in suggesting that for many years word attack has been the principal preoccupation of elementary reading instruction. The majority stress traditional phonics. Some return to the older approach of synthesis, that is, teaching the child to respond to letters sequentially, a sound at a time (buh-a-tuh). Others follow the basic reader favored analytic approach, that is, teaching the child to respond to letter substitutions in words previously learned by sight. (If *bat* is learned by sight, then the child is taught he can substitute initial and final consonants and medial vowel: *p*at, pa*d*, *pet*.) Still other supplementary phonics programs employ both the synthetic and analytic approaches.

We have had a rash of modified alphabets to lend a new look to phonics. The best known is the i.t.a. (initial teaching alphabet) with forty-four characters attempting to enhance the regularity of alphabet and sound relationships. The other modification which has attracted wide attention is "Words in Color." Here the added cue is not a new alphabet, but color added to the old alphabet. In neither case is there uncontested evidence supporting these "new looks" in phonics.

Probably the most far-reaching challenge to the prevailing modes of instruction, whether through the basic reader or through the various supplementary phonics programs just described, has been advanced by linguistic scholarship. This long-established discipline had great impact on reading instruction in the sixties. Its principal contribution to date has been a new approach to word identification. It clearly has other contributions to make through its studies of syntax, intonation, and dialect. But those contributions are coming along at a slower pace than the insights into word identification.

What can we conclude about these differing approaches to word identification: basic reader, supplementary phonics, linguistics? Jeanne Chall in *Learning to Read: The Great Debate* addressed herself to that question. Professor Chall thought that the basic difference among the approaches was a "meaning emphasis" versus a "code emphasis." By "code emphasis" she said she meant "the alphabetic code." And her conclusion?

> My analysis of the existing experimental comparisons of a meaning versus a code emphasis tends to support Bloomfield's definition that the first step in learning to read in one's native language is essentially learning a printed code for the speech we possess. It does not support the prevailing view that sees the beginning reader as a miniature adult who should, from the start, engage in mature reading. Early stress on code learning, these studies indicate, not only produces better word recognition and spelling, but also makes it easier for the child eventually to read with understanding—at least up to the beginning of the fourth grade, after which point there is practically no evidence.[3]

Jeanne Chall, in making this judgment on the teaching of word identification, is obviously being especially critical of basic readers. But to be fair to her I should also quote this qualifying statement:

> I cannot stress sufficiently that this dichotomy is only one of *emphasis*. All code-emphasis programs give some practice in reading for meaning during the initial stages. Many put great stress on it. Reading for meaning really cannot be avoided unless, of course, only nonsense syllables are used, and no code-emphasis program has ever gone to that extreme.
> Similarly, the meaning-emphasis programs give some practice in code learning. Reading could not take place without some attention to the code. But compared with code-emphasis programs, the meaning-emphasis programs provide less practice, and they give it later.[4]

It is further only fair to say that the basic readers appearing since Professor Chall's review have stronger and earlier instruction in the code. At least, so it seems to me.

Another powerful force for change in elementary reading teaching has been an intensified interest in individualization of instruction. As a first illustration, let me cite the return to the language experience approach. This way of teaching reading through child-dictated text had been popular in the thirties, culminating in a widely read book by Lillian A. Lamoreaux and Dorris May Lee, *Learning to Read through Experience*,[5] but it remained largely a supplementary medium until Roach Van Allen, then in California, stirred a kind of renascence. The book, *Language Experiences in Reading*,[6] co-authored by Van Allen and Claryce Allen, extended that concept along with commercially published guides for daily classroom use of the language experience approach as a principle, no longer supplementary, medium of instruction. The obvious vulnerability of the approach is the difficulty of insuring adequate and systematic attention to word identification and syntactical or intonational control. Of course, neither strength nor vulnerability is inevitable. The strength can be diminished, the vulnerability overcome. However, it does seem reasonable to say that the approach depends heavily, perhaps more heavily than most approaches, on the competence of the individual teaching.

Then, there is individualized reading, the program which teaches reading largely out of a variety of trade or "library" books and permits each child to select his own books and move at his own pace. The first great surge of interest in this approach came in the fifties under proponents like May Lazar of the New York City Bureau of Educational Research. Interest has continued to grow. Patrick Groff of San Diego made one review of the research on individualized reading in which it was clear that while individualized reading did not result in greater gains than ability grouping it produced at least as much achievement gain as ability groups.[7] As for me, I would have about the same comment as I had for the language experience approach: strength comes from individuality, vulnerability from problems in assuring systematic instruction in word attack, intonation, and syntax. And again, of course, the approach depends heavily on individual teaching competence.

Computer-assisted instruction, and most other technological aids, favor the idea of programmed learning. But we cannot say with assurance that the programmed approach is better than some others. The principal problem with all technological devices is cost. American ingenuity and time will solve that difficulty, I'm sure. Meanwhile, I should hope we would all be circumspect in investing large sums of money in unproven hardware. To provide funds for research in technology is one thing; to invest before the evidence is in is quite another.

I believe that interest in the differing reading tasks posed by separate subjects will grow as the separate subjects are more rigorously defined at the elementary school level. Many curriculum projects are attempting to achieve that sharper definition. You can see it most vividly in mathematics. But it is also true of the natural sciences. Definition appears to come more slowly in the social studies. And there are obviously difficulties in the language arts. Still, one promising effort in the language arts, the Nebraska Curriculum in Elementary English, is enjoying wide attention.

One approach to meeting these differing tasks of the separate subjects has been to issue readers with brief units in the disciplines. These aids may be helpful as they seem to have been at the secondary level. But it also seems reasonable to expect that the next steps must be to build this help into the day-by-day instruction within each subject. I am confident that reading assistance will become integral in all elementary school subjects.

The rate of change in materials and methods of instruction became markedly accelerated in the sixties, and all of us had some difficulty keeping a sense of perspective. I do think we should try to refrain from jumping on bandwagons at least until we have some assurance that the music is good.

Now let me talk about changes in organization for instruction. Most elementary classrooms are still self-contained. Most use the three group plan of organization. For many years we have defended this plan, assuming one and all that the groups are "flexible." I'm sure we all believe in the cruciality of flexibility. If the groups in fact are caste systems and children live and die without escape, no one can defend them. Yet if we are honest we all know that in fact flexibility is difficult to maintain. You can think of a variety of ways in which the group could be changed for reading. If we are to stay with this system of organization, let us all try to encourage it to be what we say it is.

Departmentalization has not been popular in the elementary school for a long time. We can defend its rejection only if we can ensure teaching competence not only in reading, but across the curriculum. Can we? Or, are there other general grounds on which we can justify rejection? Or, are there differing grounds at differing levels in the elementary school? Or, could we have departmentalization part of the day as in the dual progress plan of Stoddard? Whatever our answers to these questions, they ought to be something more than ideological.

And then there is team-teaching. Is it that much different

from departmentalization? Or is there some virtue not found in departmentalization? Perhaps the possibilities for varying size of group and time for instruction are more readily realizable.

What about non-graded instruction or continuous progress plans? Do these organizational schemes not depend on some kind of programmed learning for the whole curriculum? Has such programming been worked out in detail? Perhaps, even if not, the effort in this direction is worth risking some ambiguity in planning and availability of appropriate instructional materials.

In many ways the most interesting innovation in organizing for instruction is the cross-age grouping espoused by Lippitt and others. Here older children teach younger. Middle graders teach reading, for example, to primary graders. The possibilities seem promising if wisely managed.

I suppose in the last analysis none of these changes in organizational schemes is as important as a substantive analysis of the teaching tasks in reading and appropriate provision of teaching personnel and materials. But as Americans we have always been attracted to the power of management. Indeed, we may sometimes prize efficiency at the expense of significance.

Teacher judgment, informal assessments, observation of day-by-day behavior—these all have an important place and must not be lost in the assessment of reading programs. I have already said something about assessing reading readiness. And the essence of my comment was that we need surer diagnosis. I now want to extend that judgment to all the evaluation we attempt. Global assessments in reading, placing children at "grade level," conceal as much as they reveal. It is hard to know with most reading tests what to do with the results. And even the tests labelled "diagnostic" have real limitations. Most give much useful information on word identification but once we move to syntax and then beyond to connected discourse the guidance becomes considerably fuzzier. And we need, as we always have, to place standardized testing within the wider context of broad evaluations.

Let me digress with an attempt to look ahead. I believe that beginning-to-read instruction will become increasingly efficient. I think that efficiency will show first and most markedly in the instruction in word identification skills. The confluence of the new insights from linguistics and from the psychology of verbal behavior supported by the awesome data-gathering powers of the computer will not only delineate sharply the essential skills but demonstrate how to plan different kinds of strategies, tactics, and pacings for different kinds of children.

I believe basic comprehension skills will also improve. At

first the improvement will be evident at the sentence level where the suasions of syntax will be better understood. Concomitantly, I believe we will begin methods of reading attack in the separate subjects. We have started to move that way so that we now have some materials which show the differing vocabularies and the differing conceptual structures in the distinctive disciplines. But these materials, while very helpful, are a first step only. We need, and I believe will get, reading instruction built into the day-by-day teaching of the subject and interwoven with the substance of the subject.

I believe we will see increasing individualization of instruction. Again the computer will be of enormous assistance in showing what is necessary and what will work. This individualization will extend not only to over-all learning capacities but also to linguistic and cultural differences.

We will have more testing. And I believe it, too, will improve. We have always needed better instruments than we now have. The National Assessment Project headed by Ralph Tyler is a harbinger of what is to come. I hope the improved methods of appraisal will be wisely employed.

Finally, I believe that we will see in the years ahead that the arts of language belong together. Listening, speaking, reading, and writing belong in unified instruction. Full responsibility for enhancing reading competence has yet to come at the high school level, and therefore it would be more honest of me to call developments I will be discussing trends I *wish* would come in secondary reading.

But first, let me state why I believe the realities in secondary reading have to be faced more comprehensively:

1. Reading competence grows most efficiently when it is directly nurtured. If reading development after the sixth grade, indeed after any grade, is left to chance, growth is at best erratic and at worst levels off or even retrogresses.
2. At any grade level, achievement levels for any representative group of students distribute themselves over a wide range.
3. The reading materials of the high school curriculum employ vocabulary never before encountered. The syntactical elements grow increasingly complex. The ideational structures of the several disciplines call for comprehensions steadily more rigorous.

The trends I wish would come in secondary reading are these:

1. Basic continuing instruction for the median-progressing reader.

2. Complementary reading instruction in every subject.
3. Extended instruction for very able readers.
4. Intensive instruction for retarded readers.

I know all of these responsibilities have been accepted in some degree in most secondary schools. But I have come to believe the responsibilities for reading instruction must be met in fuller measure if we are to meet the rising cry of youth for changes in our schools. For the truth is, that whether the curriculum is relevant or irrelevant, it cannot be successfully communicated unless students can read.

But cannot this communication be achieved through television, radio, the motion picture? No. There is too much to be understood in depth to rely on these media alone. To paraphrase Sir Francis Bacon: Some matters are to be tasted, others to be swallowed, and some few to be chewed and digested. It is the substance of the curriculum needing to be chewed and digested that requires the thinking time only the printed word allows. In reading, if students take time for intellectual mastication and digestion, they need not worry about the substance being snatched away.

Now I am not one who feels free to add to the burdens of supervisors and teachers. On the contrary, I believe most supervisors and teachers are already overburdened. I am quite willing to say that a more complete program of instruction in reading cannot come to high schools unless some burdens are lightened. It is not my place to say which shall go and which shall stay. But it is my place to suggest that priorities might well be reviewed in this crisis time. The crucial elements in instruction need first consideration.

So, as I spell out what seems to me necessary for a full program in reading instruction for high school students, please remember that I fully recognize that no such program can be implemented without realistic readjustments in educational priorities. With that proviso, I should like to outline what might be done in the four facets of reading instruction I have named.

In the elementary school, every student receives basic reading instruction. It is called basic because the fundamental linguistic skills are taught: basic word identification skills—phonics, structure, context; basic comprehension skills—sentence patterns and connected discourse. Now let us for the moment confine ourselves to the median-developing high school student—the average student. What is the state of those skills? To answer that question, I must turn to a distinction which seems to me important. Elementary students learn their basic skills largely through story-type exercises. So I would expect the kinds of words employed in a wide variety of stories would readily be decoded. I would be confident that the sentence patterns of fiction would be under student command. I would expect students to be able to follow the structure of a story. But now let us think of the high school curriculum. Is most of the curriculum communicated through story? We all know it is not. Most of the curriculum is carried by the expository mode. In exposition, words are chosen for consensus in response. The ideal choice is that word to which sender and receiver can lend identity in meaning. Of all the curricula, mathematics exemplifies the ideal best. In exposition, sentences are patterned to achieve convergence in responses. In exposition, connected discourse is governed by logic. Deduction and induction are the prevailing structures.

At this point I should like to be sure that I am not misunderstood. I am not complaining about elementary school basic reading instruction. I am only suggesting a practical complement to what basic reading instruction tries to do. I am suggesting that basic reading instruction at the high school level might be focused where there are likely to be maximum dividends. I would like to think that literature, including fiction, ought to be taught in its own right and not as a reading skill-building medium for the rest of the curriculum. The kind of reading skill servicing the rest of the curriculum ought to be taught through exposition. Let median-developing students practice the kind of convergence the words of exposition demand. The imaginative elaboration desired from words of the literary mode through which the students have been taught in the elementary school is different. Let high school students practice the sentence patterns of exposition. The expository mode *specifies*. The sentences in stories from which they have previously been taught only suggest. Let high school students practice the logical structures of exposition. Let them appraise when a principle can be induced from the data given. The story is not a logical exercise. Think of the paragraphing in stories. How often can you, in fact, see fully wrought main idea and supporting detail? Is paragraphing in stories really consistently parallel to paragraphing, let us say, in science? Or think of mathematics. In the elementary school, the verbally-stated problem is called a "story" problem. But, whether at elementary or secondary level, is a verbal problem in mathematics really at all like a story? Is it not a compact piece of text, terse and tightly structured? Does it not require a sharp convergence in response, predetermined in comprehensive detail by the writer? Indeed is it at all functional anywhere in mathematics to indulge in a story-type response? If you are in any doubt about your answers to these questions, let me remind you that the correlation between effective performance in basic reading and effective reading in mathematics has always been low.

Please remember that I am not for a moment suggesting neglecting the further development of reading in literature. What I am suggesting is that reading in literature be thought of as requiring specialized responses—responses not fully functional in most of the rest of the curriculum. I would not want high school English classes to sacrifice any of their traditional concern for developing literary appreciation. All I am saying is that these appreciations are different from the responses sought in most of the curriculum.

The second kind of reading instruction in the high school belongs in the separate disciplines. Reading is focused by the domain of knowledge in which it is employed. To read well in any discipline is to think well in that discipline. Each discipline has a conceptual vocabulary. Each has a manner of statement. Each has structures through which it develops, applies, and appraises its ideas. Literature, social studies, science, mathematics, any discipline you wish to name, differs in some degree in the way it employs the elements of discourse.

I will illustrate this point a little further in mathematics. Mathematics operates with at least four vocabularies:

(1) a verbal symbol vocabulary
(2) a numerical symbol vocabulary
(3) a literal symbol vocabulary
(4) an operational symbol vocabulary.

Some mathematical statements use only verbal symbols: the area of a rectangle is equal to the product of its length and width. Some mathematical statements use only numerical and operational symbols: $10 \times 5 = 50$. Some mathematical statements use only literal and operational symbols: $A = lw$. Some mathematical statements mix all four vocabularies together: What is the area of a rectangle where $L = 5$ feet and $W = 10$?

In mathematical vocabulary, the referent for which each kind of symbol stands has to be clear before the student can use the symbol to advantage. This advantage is difficult enough to achieve when using any one kind of symbol, let alone four. It is grossly analogous to a man who mixes English, Spanish, German, and French in the same statement.

Mathematics not only operates with four vocabularies but all these vocabularies demand the most specified response. Tolerance for individualistic response is ordinarily not permitted in mathematical vocabulary. Even when common words are employed as mathematical symbols, they acquire a new exactitude.

Then, the number vocabulary of mathematics demands a different response to its separate symbols, much more highly specified, than is expected to the separate symbols of a word. The response to separate numbers when grouped is determined by place value ($1, 2, 3, 4$); the response to separate letters when grouped is determined by sound value (word).

Whereas context is often a serviceable guide to the meaning of an unknown word in most disciplines, it functions very ineffectively in mathematics. Mathematical statement is so economical that for the most part each symbol is self-contained. That is, other symbols do not provide the kind of clues to meaning found in most fields of learning. Thus, the reader in mathematics must carry to the symbol the necessary context knowing he will not get much help from the surrounding in which it is embedded.

Finally, vocabulary in mathematics demands operational competence as part of response. It is not enough to define a term, the student must be able to put the symbol to its appropriate uses.

Beyond vocabulary, all mathematical statement requires efficiently achieved, specified responses about the relationships being communicated. Almost any other discipline is more redundant and hence offers more than one chance at relevant response. Mathematicians aim to say no more and no less than is intended. Every word and symbol in a statement has a particular purpose and no necessary word or symbol is lacking.

As the reader moves from statement to connected discourse, he must quickly get a sense of structure. He does not have a paragraph or more to apprise him gradually of the shape of things to come. Moreover, the reader must use the same terse text for a number of purposes. First, as we have said, he must obtain a sense of general relationships: the structure of the problem. Next, he must decide upon the processes appropriate to that structure. Then he must note and use the quantitative data in the processes whether expressed in words, numbers, or letters. At this point he may need to check to see that he has read efficiently and has neither missed some essential of structure, nor failed to see a necessary operation, nor overlooked some quantitative detail. This kind of intensive re-reading is demanded almost nowhere else.

This discussion illustrates that the competence in meeting the reading tasks of a discipline really can be gained only within the context of the discipline. This holds true not only for mathematics, but also for literature, social studies, science, and any other discipline.

The third kind of reading instruction needed in high schools is reading development for the very able. Very able readers ought to feel the exciting intellectual demands when a task is just barely within their grasp. Only by stretching—hard—can they reach it at all. The task should be built upon competence developed within the several disciplines. If able readers have been shown how to read effectively within the separate subjects, they will be ready to put these approaches to use to gain comprehensive insights rising about specialized knowledge.

I suggest these readers then be gathered in liberal arts seminars. The seminars might very well set their own areas of surveillance: some around issues which all undertake to investigate, others around problems which an individual wishes to undertake on his own. Of course, high standards of performance would be expected. Materials on quite mature levels would have to be available. Reporting, analyzing, writing, would sharpen the edge of competence as the students read.

Vocabulary development would arise out of the common areas of investigation as well as from the individual projects. Students would be encouraged to enjoy the conceptual tools a working vocabulary brings. They would view the etymology of words, the history of the language which words reflect. They would discuss precision in usage, connotations and denotations, large and small. Word study need not be dull. After all, words are the tools of thought.

Beyond vocabulary, the able reader's principal instruction would be in critical reading. The late Professor Gray of the University of Chicago used to think of reading as progressing through four stages:

1. Securing literal meanings
2. Obtaining implied meanings
3. Reacting to literal and implied meaning
4. Using reactions as part of further reading, indeed as part of all learning.

The emphasis with these very able readers would of course be on the third and fourth stages: reacting and using. Their keen minds would be further sharpened against the best thinking—new and old—available through their reading. They would analyze, qualify, extend, and apply what they read. Part of this exercise in critical thinking would arise in seminar give-and-take. Part would be invested in individual written critique.

Again, the seminar for able readers should not be devoted to any one field of knowledge. It should be a "liberal arts" seminar ranging widely among many disciplines, putting to rigorous use the abilities in reading developed earlier within the disciplines. For further specific approaches, may I call your attention to the recent excellent book, edited by Martha King and her associates at Ohio State University, called *Critical Reading*? [8]

The high school has paid the most attention to remedial reading. The principal task in remedial reading is to get students to try again. What these students need to learn is what their brethren learned in the primary grades. They need to learn how to identify words through phonics, structure, context, use of the dictionary. They need to learn how to group words together in sentences, how to group sentences together in paragraphs, how to group paragraphs together in more extended discourse. These skills are no different from the skills learned earlier by their brethren. Of course, the material through which remediation is sought must not affront the student. He is not a primary child and cannot be treated as one.

Beyond these language skills, the remedial reader needs mostly instruction in the approaches demanded by the separate subjects. Most of this responsibility cannot be carried by the remedial reading teacher; it must fall to the English teacher, the social studies teacher, the science teacher, the mathematics teacher. In other words, what we must face in the high school about remedial reading is this: if the student is truly in need of remediation in reading, he is in need of remediation through his whole program of studies. It will not do to build his morale a little in a reading class and then crush his spirit through the rest of the day.

Remedial reading teachers are wonderful people. They devote themselves to their hard, frustrating tasks with remarkable devotion. They have always deserved the highest admiration. But no reading teacher can haul a student struggling with beginning reading skills through all he must learn. The remedial reading teacher must have comrades in arms in every subject we want the student to learn. I know this kind of program—total remediation—is very difficult to manage. Yet I know no satisfactory alternative. I should be quite irresponsible if I even suggested that the best taught remedial reading would solve all the students' learning problems. If we really want to face the problem honestly, we must remediate in every class every day. I do not pretend that is easy. I do assert it is the only way the problem can be mastered.

How easy it is for me to describe the trends I wish would come in secondary reading. How much more difficult it is to move wishes into realities. The desired realities will not come in the immediate future even if everyone endorses the wishes. Yet I do believe it crucial that all teachers look to the long-term, however difficult, goal of assuming full responsibility for reading instruction in the high school.

1. N. L. Gage, *Handbook of Research on Teaching* (Chicago: Rand McNally & Company, 1963).

2. Robert C. Calfee and Richard L. Venezky, *Component Skills in Beginning Reading* (Madison, Wisconsin: University of Wisconsin, Research and Development Center for Cognitive Learning, 1968); and Robert C. Calfee, R. Chapman, and R. L. Venezky, "How a Child Needs to Learn to Think to Learn to Read," in *Cognition in Learning and Memory*, edited by L. Greg (New York: Wiley, forthcoming).

3. Jeanne Chall, *Learning to Read: The Great Debate* (New York: McGraw-Hill Book Company, 1967), p. 83. Reprinted by permission of the author.

4. Ibid., p. 137.

5. Lillian A. Lamoreaux and Dorris May Lee, *Learning to Read through Experience* (New York: Appleton-Century-Crofts, Inc., 1943).

6. Roach Van Allen and Claryce Allen, *Language Experiences in Reading* (Chicago: Encyclopaedia Britannica Educational Corporation, 1966).

7. Patrick J. Groff, "Comparisons of Individualized and Ability Grouping Approach in Teaching Reading," *Elementary English*, Vol. 41 (March 1964), pp. 238-241.

8. Martha L. King (ed.), et al., *Critical Reading* (Philadelphia: J. B. Lippincott Company, 1967).

*Grades and corrections have no place in rehabilitative programs. Indeed, since grades and corrections have usually caused the mischief in the first place, their reinstatement at any point is suspect. Value attached to what is strong, clear, honest, and individual is the most potent teacher.*

# Children, Composing, Creativity, and Computers

## by Alvina Treut Burrows

Ours is a computerized era. Computer-planned romances are frequent in current anecdotes; some few are really serious. Universities and public schools find increasingly valuable the time-saving aspects of the computer. But it will be a long time before the computer will do much to aid children's composing directly. It would be foolish, however, to resist the idea of computer-aided instruction just as it was foolish to resist printed books in the early days of the printing press.

Long as my title is, let me reshape it to fit the "mod mode" of this computer era somewhat as follows: "Children, Teachers, Children, Teachers, Creativity, Children, Computers, Children, Teachers, Composing, Teachers, Children!" Repetition and attempted simultaneity in this wording reflect the fact that writing is a distinctly human affair, done *by* people and *for* people. The

**Dr. Alvina T. Burrows**
Professor of Elementary Education
New York University

emphasis is appropriate, I believe, for a group of leaders to consider. Computers? Yes, for they can tell us much about the nature of language, and the many items that can be analysed in children's writing and about the processes by which they compose. But our concern, here and now, is with teachers and children and the creativity that they both inject into composing.

Let us look at written composition using ourselves as mirrors. How many teachers do we know who have written a story, an essay, a poem, or even a scrap of a dramatic episode in the last six months? How many have written a letter-to-the-editor or one to their Congressman expounding their views on some crucial current issue? How many have written, *voluntarily*, an informative account of the success in their states or cities in teaching students to read or to listen to the fine books of our Golden Age of Children's Literature? Certainly, such items are dramatic and needed in many local newspapers or teachers' journals. I suspect that we can think of only a very few who have written anything *they did not have to write* in the last year.

Teachers and other adults give lack of time most frequently as an excuse for their avoidance of writing. But these same people admit that they find time to sing or to play a musical instrument, to garden, to paint, to model with clay. Fear of writing, pervasive and corroding, stops the urge to put oneself on paper in words, the most available of all media. "Self-expression," or even written persuasion to insights of great personal significance rarely reach written commitment. Search for reasons for this fear always reveals a central cause: low grades in school composition courses, negative criticisms, red-penciled corrections and the demand to "write it over again" have destroyed the urge to write and have destroyed it effectively.

Can teachers who fear and avoid writing teach children to write with joy and self-confidence or even with basic clarity? Can attitudes toward writing be changed in teachers, old or new? How do some teachers help children retain both the desire and the daring to write? Can "correctness" be learned without sacrificing imagination, fluency, and a sense of power over words? Can one grow in many of the aspects of writing without destroying the ego? Can writing give wholesome nourishment for a wholesome self?

Only a few answers are at hand but more are emerging; still others are indicated by reflection upon our own teaching experiences and upon the nature of our language.

### Do Teachers' Attitudes Toward Writing Affect Children?

Research has not yet yielded precise answers to the gnawing inquiry into the contagion of the teachers' attitudes toward writing. Every "hunch" suggests that attitudes are caught in the classroom as effectively as at home. And even if teachers' fears do not demonstrably affect children, their often deflating comments and corrections on children's papers do the job, and do it thoroughly. Furthermore, composing, which should be directed toward an audience, usually of one's peers, is subverted to an exercise for the approval of a single power-wielding adult. The process becomes a minimal effort to "get by."

## Can Teachers' Attitudes Toward and Power in Writing Be Enhanced?

The answer to this topical question is YES, but not easily! Observation supports the possibility of continuous human change and development, but little research on adult growth in composition is at hand. However, that little is encouraging. Ramon Veal found that a sample of 49 elementary teachers enrolled in an NDEA Institute at the University of Georgia showed statistically significant gains as measured by two tests separated by a summer of composition work. He used different forms of the STEP Essay Test for college freshmen and sophomores.[1]

Informed observation adds samples of mature teachers belatedly achieving satisfaction from writing for local professional magazines or for project reports. That this delayed achievement is possible at all suggests that it could happen much more often.

## How Can Adult Non-Composers Be Rehabilitated?

How can a staff of professional leaders—supervisors, consultants, directors—set about changing teachers' attitudes and assisting their growth in writing? Workshops and institutes[2] are probably the most immediate means of helping teachers achieve this goal, as well as other professional goals. Guides have been carefully planned for such institutes in English. The many points of view are invaluable.

The importance of informality and of leader-student rapport must be constantly reenforced. Evaluation must be postponed, except for the evaluation inherent in encouragement. When group members comment favorably upon some vivid phrase, a revealing example, or a powerfully built piece of persuasion, they are *attaching value* to that instance. This kind of evaluation is needed again and again. Fluency and courage must be built before even an adult learner is ready for vigorous analysis. Anonymous contributions to class readings are often a first offering. Noting that at least one quality has merit often spurs the novice to further effort. A frequent source of compositions for such class response is the daily journal of private and random writing from which the author selects an occasional item to refine and to submit for class use. As confidence grows, students go from anonymous status to willing identification of their own papers.

Grades and corrections have no place in rehabilitative programs. Indeed, since grades and corrections have usually caused the mischief in the first place, their reinstatement at any point is suspect. Value attached to what is strong, clear, honest, and individual is the most potent teacher.

## Contributive stimuli

Analysis of writing should be confined to the writing of professionals during institutes or workshops. Appreciating how experts achieve clarity or vividness or details to amass a crescendo of feeling or a sense of immediacy adds to awareness in responding to literature and to the student's reservoir—perhaps unconscious—of experimental techniques within his own writing. Beyond the occasional analysis of certain examples of effective writing, wide reading of many kinds of literature also adds, though slowly, to the student's writing power. So, too, do spontaneous dramatization—without an audience, of course—dramatic reading, listening to poetry recorded by experts and reading good verse aloud in the "class" by the students themselves for one another and in small groups. Discussing films and plays as well as their observations of people and events currently of significance to them also has value. These many stimuli are as necessary for development of skill in writing as is the writing experience itself. In the process of un-learning destructive attitudes and relearning constructive ones, the adult needs literature in non-defensive contacts and many ways to see, think, and express himself. Equally needed is a live, receptive audience to whom his written and oral communication speaks.

The techniques cited take time, and there are no short cuts. Attitudes of long standing can not be made over by pressure tactics. Crash courses will not wipe out years of self-doubt. Excessive demands that foster superficiality at best and dishonesty at worst are long remembered. The inarticulate verbal fumblings that result from such assignments are not easily replaced. Prevention of negative learnings is the desideratum in both liberal arts and teachers colleges rather than expensive therapy.

## Children's composing

In courses devoted to teaching the language arts, a generous exposure to juvenile composing with many materials is a clear necessity. Observing children's joy in writing in schools in which their writing, painting, sculpture, and music are cordially received is more convincing than exhortations to treat child products with respect. Video tape enables whole classes of prospective teachers to view and to view again productive occasions of children's writing with on-the-spot vividness.

Writing done to inform, convince, or to raise questions is concerned at best with objective data. It meets the public eye by being posted, duplicated, bound into a book for the classroom library, or sent directly to a recipient. Out of deference to its "public," correct form is in order. Such correction can best take place in a teacher-pupil conference or in a pupil-partner conference which the teacher later re-checks. (Most sentence errors, especially incomplete or run-on sentences, are corrected by listening for terminal voicing as children read aloud to each other, or to the teacher, and make their punctuation match their aural skill.) Discussion of such factual writing, as in the case of a report or persuasive essay, results in class discussion of *content*, not of correctness. Change in the reader is the test. Clear, vigorous writing presents convincing data leading to change in the audience—to questions, plans, or, conversely, to rebuttal. The test of excellence is the behavior of the respondents, not in the proper sequence of tenses or in correct spelling. Editing with a teacher, or fellow pupil for some purposes, can correct needed items before the paper is visually available to its public. Editing a few pieces of writing for public consumption is a far different thing from correcting nearly every "composition" for the sake of certain rules or to get a passing grade.

Another realm of writing of equal importance generally and of even greater importance to young children is that of imaginative narrative and verse. In freely experimental situations, children produce these two forms overwhelmingly more than others. Here the goal is to entertain a live and well-known audience. Even less "correcting" is in order than in the factual and more practical field noted above. In *They All Want to Write*, Alvina T. Burrows discusses the case of Katie, who dictated the two stories which follow, first from eagerness to do what her friends were enjoying, and secondly from the sense of power that their approval gave her.

> Once there was a little girl and her mother. They didn't have any money. So they had to go out and look everywhere, but they couldn't find any. Then the little girl saw a box under a bush, and she looked in and there was a *lot* of money—one thousand sixty-seven gold dollars! So they took it to the store and got all the things they wanted.[3]

In this story Katie almost openly imitated the invention her second grade friends were using; her main addition to a familiar plot was the element of *gold* money and that in gratifying quantity! The class was impressed by such a find.

Just a few weeks later, Katie dictated another story. This time, the recall of her previous one triggered her acceptance of the teacher's invitation. Note the emergence of a little more plot structure (but only a little) and of mischief curtailed with both reasonableness and humor.

> Once there was a kitten named White Paws because, of course, he had white paws. Well, one day he jumped on the desk and knocked a bottle of ink on the floor. And he walked all around in the ink and all over the carpet. So they had to call him Black Paws, and he had to stay outside after that.[4]

Katie continued to dictate and to write on her own throughout the year, revealing the unevenness of growth characteristic of children and of creative expression generally. No one would have dreamed from her first story that Katie would be able to dictate the following short verse, remarkable for its imagery and for its storm-like strength.

> Lightning,
> Who made you?
> Did some great giant
> Write you with a flashing pen?
> Did he? [5]

But even more important than this striking surge of imaginative response was Katie's new courage to experiment with verbal and other composition and her new confidence in her own powers.

Dictated stories and verse present no problems of correction. They are written from dictation by the teacher and treasured by the composer in his own private folder. Skill in handwriting grows from composing and sometimes copying brief dictated letters, notes, memos, and captions, and from the minimal writing necessary to spelling, arithmetic, and other curricular learnings. Independence emerges gradually over several years and at vastly different rates for different pupils. In time, children grow in their control over characters on paper. This new strength results from appreciative class response, from widened literary reading, from dramatic invention, and from spontaneous acting out of many kinds of characters. The following story suggests emerging ability to handle characters of different kinds and their interaction.

## The Five Chipmunks Turn Peddler [6]

One day Chippy, Chappy, Chopper, Munch, and Dart were playing out in the yard when they heard somebody's footsteps coming down the road. So they ran out of the yard to see who was coming and guess what was coming? A peddler with a tremendous bundle on his back.

The five chipmunks ran in the house to tell Mother about who was coming. Just as the peddler came to their door the five chipmunks raced to the door and there stood the peddler. He had a ragged cloak. You couldn't see what color it was. He sold Mother Chipmunk some pots and pans, some napkins, and a table cloth with some fringe around it.

That night the five had an idea to run away and turn peddler. They packed their clothes and jumped out of the window—all except Munch who was scared. So Chopper had to carry him. Chopper nearly fell down. After Munch was down they ran down the road to catch up with the peddler. Finally they did.

The next morning Mother Chipmunk went upstairs calling, "Children! Breakfast!"

No answer.

"Breakfast!"

No answer.

By this time she was really mad. "Children, I know you're kidding. Come on!"

No answer.

So Mother Chipmunk went into their room. There wasn't anybody in the room. Mother Chipmunk fainted. Father Chipmunk came up the stairs. His glasses fell off.

Meanwhile the five chipmunks were getting tired of walking so they said to the peddler, "Let's stop walking."

But the peddler said, "No."

The five chipmunks said, "We are going home." So they ran home as fast as they could.

They sat down at the table and said, "Never again will we run away."

### THE END

In this well-fashioned tale, a fourth grader projected the age-old yearning to run away from parental restrictions, but he did it with perceptible freshness of characterization. He and his friends wrote many stories about the chipmunk family, adding new dimensions of character to their familiar protagonists. The author's delight in putting adults into ridiculous postures was not lost upon his nine-year-old audience. That this story was written in a community in which door-to-door peddling was unknown added a novel element, drawn perhaps from reading and imagination. Action is crammed into the mounting tension of Mother's calling her children to breakfast. Both the economy and the humor of this passage were enjoyed by the class and, obviously, by the author.

## Children as audience and as authors

But even if the story had been a poor one, it would have been graciously received. There are loose ends in the peddler story: Mother and Father are left in limbo as is the peddler himself. Only the juveniles are in at the finale! But to offer remedial suggestion here would have been useless. The characters, with their vigor, their foibles, and their humor, had entertained the listeners. Enough!

It is sometimes difficult to find even one quality to approve in a child's story, but it is always worth the effort to try. At least a character's name or size, or a colorful phrase, a warm or pleasant feeling implied rather than told or a surprise (and children's stories are full of surprises) can be found. Not praise in general or insincerely glowing statements but comment upon a specific happening or person or turn of phrase—these open the way for growth. To spur children on to further writing is to reenforce the possibility for growth; to inhibit writing by indifference or negative response is to preclude growth. Children, alternating roles from time to time as authors and listeners, come to see that they all write more and better when they search for things to enjoy in their stories than when they look for weaknesses to correct. The latter is dreadfully easy, and it almost always discourages free and abundant writing.

### Continued Writing for Continued Growth

The foregoing capsule gives only a hint of the satisfaction and power that emerge when minimal correction is applied only to writing that is to be published. (Teachers themselves should have experienced this satisfaction and pleasure in their pre-teaching education so that their adult years would have been enriched by truly adult literacy.) Then, too, teachers should observe children's writing and assist them in developing power in the two major categories of writing; practical (largely objective) and personal (largely subjective). A small but growing number of schools, pioneering in creative experiences for fifty years in this country, have led the way to understanding some of the dimensions of children's growth in writing.

1. Ramon M. Veal, *An Evaluation of Participants' Writing Improvement During an NDEA English Institute,* a paper read at the Chicago meeting of the NCTE, February 19, 1966.

2. National Council of Teachers of English, *Source Book on English Institutes for Elementary Teachers* (Urbana, Illinois: National Council of Teachers of English, 1965).

3. Alvina Treut Burrows, D. C. Jackson, and D. O. Saunders, *They All Want to Write: Written English in the Elementary School* (New York: Holt, Rinehart and Winston, Inc., 1964), p. 143. Reprinted by permission of the publisher.

4. Ibid., p. 143.

5. Ibid., p. 145.

6. Alvina Treut Burrows, R. G. Stauffer, and D. C. Jackson, *American English*, Book IV (New York: Holt, Rinehart and Winston, Inc., 1961), pp. 252-253. Reprinted by permission of the publisher.

*. . . curriculum workers in the social studies are following the mathematics-science model with much more success than are those in the English language arts. . . . The people in the English language arts are having a more difficult time defining their area and finding basic principles with enough intellectual mileage to carry the student to the heart of the structure of the subject. National commissions on the teaching of English cannot now reach agreement about what is English. Only those scholars who find most of the answers in the field of linguistics are finding the math-science model helpful.*

# Current Curriculum Development and the Communications Skills

## by J. Harlan Shores

For our purposes consider that the communications skills are those of reading, writing, speaking and listening. Some persons like to include observation; others tend to point out that one communicates in mathematical terms and in the fine and applied arts. But we will have our hands full if we stick to the four most commonly accepted areas.

Before looking at these communications skills in terms of current curriculum developments, let us draw a few lines around

**Dr. J. Harlan Shores**
Professor of Elementary Education
College of Education
University of Illinois

117

current curriculum developments. Most of what we find as major concerns now had their antecedents at least a decade ago. But, except for purposes of illustration, we will go back into the history of curriculum developments no more than ten years. Ideas that are current are those that are of concern now, that may have begun to develop ten years or more ago, and that may be of even more concern in 1980.

People regard curricula in different ways. To some, the curriculum is as broad as education. They include in their concept all the experiences of children and all that influences these experiences. For our purposes we will talk only about curriculum developments as those experiences deliberately planned for children by the school—a very small part of a child's education, but the part that is our job and our area of expertness.

Chronologically in current curriculum development, 1957 makes a good starting place. This marks the advent of Sputnik I and the frenzied efforts of our government to provide assurance that we would be second to no nation in the areas of science and mathematics. These, of course, are not communications skills, but the activities in these areas definitely set the pattern for current developments in the social studies and in the English language arts. In order to understand what seems to be happening to the communications skills, we would do well to look at the mathematics-science model. Before this time (1957) research and development funds were rather difficult to get, even for these respected fields of inquiry, and even from the national government or the large industrial foundations.

Those few who had been doing research in science and mathematics before 1957 obviously had no trouble later getting federal funds from either the National Science Foundation or the U.S. Office of Education to further develop their programs. Their efforts were quickly paralleled by other groups who formed the Physical Science Study Committee, the School Mathematics Study Group, the Biological Sciences Curriculum Study, Project English, and many others less generally publicized.

These developments, as a group, probably were the greatest and most exciting influences on the curriculum since the progressive education controversy centered about the Activity Curriculum ended in the early 1940s. Each of these efforts in science and mathematics involved a reselection of content for these basic subjects. Its primary and sometimes sole justification was that this new content was better mathematics or better science than that which had been taught earlier. What made it better was that it was truer to the structure of the subject.

The reselection of content in science and mathematics was well underway and some of these demonstration programs were widely used before Jerome Bruner produced *The Process of Education* and became the best known apologist for this view. Content should emphasize the structure of a subject. In his words this involves "understanding it in a way that permits many other things to be related to it meaningfully. To learn structure, in short, is to learn how things are related." [1] J. Myron Atkin calls this "intellectual mileage." To emphasize structure is to select those ideas with the most mileage—those that will carry a student farthest into the subject.

The efforts of these groups are notable in several respects. First, they are notable in their own right for the changes they brought about. Physics, chemistry, biological science, and mathematics at both elementary and secondary levels are different in content in many schools today. They are notable, also, for the speed with which these changes occurred. Big money, mass produced materials, and federally funded institutes for in-service education make the old adage that it takes a half century or more to bring about an educational change simply untrue.

As important perhaps as the changes in science and mathematics curricula put into effect in schools is the pattern they established for curriculum development. With the help or leadership of subject specialists, the formula was first to examine the structure of the discipline: first, select the basic principles with the most intellectual mileage; second, build a sequential instructional program, including materials, around these principles; and third, try out the program and materials in selected schools, revise as necessary, and initiate it broadly through institutes. It is important to recognize that these are demonstrations rather than controlled research and that this general formula is being followed even now with less lavish support in the reselection of content in the social sciences and English language arts.

Another notable observation about this widespread emphasis upon content reselection in terms of the structure of subjects is the challenge it afforded to accepted criteria for content selection. While some authorities in the curriculum had long recognized that one criterion for the selection of content was its significance to an organized field of knowledge, most curriculum specialists emphasized three other criteria. These were: (1) it must be in keeping with and help to develop the democratic ideals and the moral commitment of all teachers and administrators in this society; (2) the content must be in keeping with the social realities, i.e., it must reflect society as it is, not as it was fifty to one hundred years ago and not even with much wishful thinking about what it might be in another few generations; and (3) it must be in keeping with accepted principles of the psychology of learning and child growth and development, i.e., simply, recognition of the fact that the content must be learned and must be functional in the life of the learner.

If one were to examine any dozen of the better established books in curriculum development, these three standards would be emphasized. I make something of it here because not one of the three is seriously considered in the recent and current emphasis upon reselection of content in the elementary and secondary schools. Instead, the single criterion used is whether the subject matter is significant to the organized field in which it belongs. Is it good mathematics? Is it good science? Is it good economics? Is it good English? Please don't misunderstand. I'm not favoring the teaching of bad mathematics or English. But I want this new content to be more than the satisfaction of the fondest dreams of a mathematician or a scholar in English. I want also to have it functional in building a better individual and social life. And, in the case of the social studies, I want it to teach and apply the democratic ideals.

Curriculum workers have for some time been faced with choices of content in mathematics and science reselected in order to achieve understanding of the underlying principles that give structure to these subjects. Similar choices now face us in the social studies and English language arts. If we accept this content, several related issues emerge: How do we tailor fundamental knowledge to the interests and capacities of children? Will it work for the mentally retarded? For the culturally disadvantaged? Is this content to prepare *all* children for the individual and social realities of our time? Is it good general education?

The eruptions from this ground swell in the reselection of content seem to be passing through three stages. First there is an action stage during which the new program is developed and put into effect. The steps in this were described earlier. Then there is a reaction stage when its strengths and shortcomings are discovered through longer and wider use. Finally, there is a synthesis stage where the best of the new and the best of the old are joined in a program better than either offered alone. Most of the social science and language arts programs are in the action stage. Many of the science programs are in the reaction stage, and the mathematics programs have begun the synthesis stage.

It seems to me that curriculum workers in the social studies are following the mathematics-science model with much more success than are those in the English language arts. The only basic problems in adapting the model to the social studies are those of deciding which social science disciplines to use as a basis for emphasis upon structure and how to combine and relate the basic principles selected. The people in the English language arts are having a more difficult time defining their area and finding basic principles with enough intellectual mileage to carry the student to the heart of the structure of the subject. National commissions on the teaching of English cannot now reach agreement about what English is. Only those scholars who find most of the answers in the field of linguistics are finding the math-science model helpful.

If curriculum theory had made a clear distinction between skill subjects and content subjects, curriculum specialists in English might find their task simplified. English at both elementary and secondary levels has no content except literature and grammar. I refer here to both the new and the traditional grammar—the study of the structure of the language. All the rest of English is skills, and the development of skills does not lend itself to the same patterns of subject-matter selection that have recently been used in the content fields. When selecting content in literature and linguistics or grammar, we might do well to search for fundamental principles basic to the structure of the discipline. We might select these, at least in part, because they are most significant to these organized fields of knowledge. With the communications skills, the principle of utility is of utmost concern. A child must understand something about the process of reading, writing, speaking and listening in order to do it well, but we aren't seeking in-depth knowledge for children about the process. The real test is whether the student can read, write, speak and listen well enough to serve his purposes in living, and ours in further instruction.

The trap of not making a clear cut distinction between skill and content areas is not a new one in English. For years we have tried to use the content of formal grammar in order to teach children to write and speak. It didn't work, and the National Council of Teachers of English has collected more than fifty years of research evidence proving that it didn't work. As a consequence this august group, which surely couldn't be accused of lowering standards in its field of specialization, has for the past fifteen years been discouraging the teaching of formal grammar in the elementary school. The fact that we still teach formal grammar in elementary schools makes one wonder about how influential research findings and the pronouncements of prestige sources are in influencing practice, but this is another matter. It is altogether likely that the teaching of formal grammar or linguistics probably will have little effect upon the ability to read, write, speak or listen at any educational level.

There are, however, two good justifications for teaching about the structure of the English language. The first of these is that linguistics is a legitimate content field and probably is as important to scholarship in language as basic mathematical concepts are to scholarship in mathematics. The second is that some knowledge of linguistics enables the kind of understanding in language that may be useful in analyzing and improving one's own writing. If it has utility in the improvement of reading, speech, and listening, I have yet to see these functional applications. It should be clear that this opinion about the general nonutility of linguistics as an avenue for skill development does not mean that the trend toward using linguistics will be reversed. It just means that I am predicting that the new grammar won't be any more functional in developing the communications skills than was the old grammar.

I have pleaded here for a clear separation in curriculum theory between skill and content subjects. This was done with full realization that the skill and content fields always function together and with the further realization that improvement in the communications skills will almost surely result in improved content learnings and vice versa. Only in pedagogy do we read about reading, write about writing, speak about speaking or listen about listening. One reads, writes, speaks and listens about the content fields—about the social studies, science, mathematics, health, art and music.

It is important to realize that any restriction of the content applications of the skills of communication weakens the skill development program. To tie the skills together in a curriculum package without content is almost like bundling a group of parasites together and saying, "Now live on each other." The skills can't live without good strong content worth reading about, worth writing and speaking about, and worth listening to. The relationship of skills to content isn't really a parasitic one because good practice of the skills strengthens rather than weakens the content learnings. The relationship skills and content enjoy is more like the symbiotic one in biology where the snake and the gopher share the same burrow to the advantage of both.

When the communications skills are taught in a subject called English without any infusion of content from other fields, there is bound to be a weakened skills program. The combination of literature and grammar cannot provide the rich opportunities needed for reading, writing, speaking and listening. If content from other fields is brought into the reading and language arts programs of the elementary school or into the English program at the secondary level, an interesting dualism develops. The skills are emphasized in the reading and language sections, and if the skill program is successful much content is learned. To learn to read without comprehension, to write without expressing good content ideas, to speak without knowing what we are talking about, or to listen without comprehension, is no accomplishment. So when these skills are taught and practiced well with content materials, the content is also learned. A good answer in the elementary school is to have the same teacher teaching both skills and content in a self-contained classroom organization. Then the only problem is one of talking to oneself about coordinating the skill and content efforts. In a departmentalized organization with subject specialists, I see no alternative but that of close cooperative planning between skill and content teachers. They will have to learn from each other or the child will be caught up in their differences.

It is interesting to note that our present concern with the culturally disadvantaged is a force which seems to run contrary to the emphasis upon cognition and intellectual excellence noted earlier. Those who see almost unlimited promise from attention to the structure of subjects are now trying hard to retool their content for deprived children. Their assumption is that these fundamental principles provide the best treatment for everyone if we just change the dosage and administer it differently. Others are digging up truths about interests and needs of children and the "whole child" concept and are looking at these as if they were not part and parcel of progressive education during the 1930s and of all good education since. Many are saying that the best key to unlocking the blockages in the education of the disadvantaged lies in the communications skills. Quite a number of new things are being tried here and we should watch them closely, not only for possible answers to problems of the disadvantaged, but for new approaches to teaching communications skills to all children.

Taking the calculated risk of sounding like an old fuddy duddy by saying that "there is nothing new under the sun," let me say that caring for deviant portions of the population is not a new problem. With the culturally disadvantaged we need new insights, new understandings, new materials, and perhaps new methods, but we do not need a new approach to the problem. These children are different. Some of them are so markedly different that they baffle the best child psychologists, but the core of the problem is the same. It is the age-old concern for the most knotty and the most important problem in education, that of adequately caring for individual differences. The answer lies in careful diagnosis and prescription for individual children, including, of course, children who are culturally disadvantaged.

Increased attention is also being given to some of the psychological aspects of communication. It has long been realized that communication is a two-way process. This is apparent in the way the communications skills are paired. One writes for someone to read, and listening is the receiving end of speaking. But more than this, communication involves rapport—a willingness to receive as well as a willingness to give. A hostile audience hears but doesn't listen, looks but doesn't read. A receptive audience identifies with the speaker or author. There is a feeling that he understands, that he is talking to me in my language. Good politicians don't miss many bets here, and good friends communicate much with a look or a gesture .

When I was earning part of my way through college by driving a truck, I knew the truck drivers' language well. I doubt that I could communicate with them now, and this is too bad. I learned the language of the university professor, but I lost the language of the truck driver, and I have never learned the language of today's teenager. I expect that those who communicate best know many languages within English and develop rapport in all of them. Perhaps our programs limited to standard English are too narrow. It may be that those best educated in the communications skills have gotten this education beyond the schools. When we try to stamp out non-standard patterns we may be weakening a communications strength—one that lets the student be one with his family and his friends. In Hawaii during the summer of 1967 I found much concern over pidgin English as this relates to the reading and language program. But many of the teachers there believe as I do, that the best avenue is not to *replace* pidgin but to *supplement* it with standard English—to teach a *second* language rather than a *single* language.

Other psychological considerations of some concern relate to the self-image of those communicating—an assuredness and freedom from fear that is important to both the sending and the receiving roles. Early and repeated successes are vital in all learning, but they seem especially so in the communications skills.

Two years ago I was spending quite a bit of time in a sixth-grade classroom in connection with a program designed to teach basic study skills. On the occasion of one classroom visit one boy had been a problem to classroom control all day and continued to irritate the teacher with minor disturbances into the afternoon social studies lesson. He was talking to a friend while the teacher was starting to develop a time line on the chalk board. In exasperation the teacher said, "Art, you seem to have a lot to say today and I can't be heard while you are talking. Perhaps you had better come up here and explain this time line." The boy was a bit embarrassed, but he was also bright and able and more than a little bored with this overview of a lesson that he had already studied. So with the whispered encouragement of a few friends, he accepted the challenge and explained the time line at the board. I'm sure that the teacher was now embarrassed and a little angry at the backfiring of a classroom control technique, but the boy knew that he could do a good job. He did it well and the teacher was enough of an old hand to swallow her anger and compliment him on the job. She then pointed out that she and the entire class had listened while he spoke and suggested that he show the same courtesy to others. He didn't disturb the class for the rest of the day, but more importantly, he achieved a language victory in a difficult situation. It was one of a long series of successes that had built a self-assuredness uncommon even among adults.

Another current curriculum development has been a sluggish movement of modern technology into education. While our lives have changed markedly in how we buy groceries, cook, wash clothes, and travel, there really hasn't been much change in how we teach. In most schools we use films and filmstrips, tapes, and radio and TV occasionally and incidentally. We may use a bit of programmed learning here and there and sometimes a language laboratory or the facilities of a learning materials center, but none of these nor any combination of them has seriously challenged the basal textbook as an organizing center for instruction in most schools. It seems as if education has been in a deep bay of the technological revolution and only occasionally feels the flow from the main current affecting nearly everything else we do. I am not chastising teachers for not using the "hardware" more. Very little of it was developed with our needs in mind and it is often more trouble than it is worth.

But this situation is now changing. A main channel of technology is now cutting a path through our placid bay. The huge electronic companies have now entered the field of education. Among these are Xerox, IBM, General Electric, RCA, Raytheon and Sylvania. With an eye on the $50 billion a year now being spent for public education at all levels, they are ready to produce both the "hardware" and the "software" for teaching. When the impact of this combined effort of funds from the federal government and big industry hits the schools with full force, teaching and learning will be changed in all schools.

This industrial revolution in education will hit both the content and skill subjects, but the largest initial efforts will probably go to the largest market, and what school is not concerned with the communications skills? The skill areas are natural ones for systems engineering leaning heavily upon communications research. Interrelated aspects of the English language arts lend themselves well to systems engineering, and the heavy emphasis upon skill-drill, or practice, will be much easier to program than are content fields where the cognitive structures are more complicated.

Industries' contributions to education to date have tended to be in terms of mass education. Educational TV, films, filmstrips, the radio, mock ups, models, and transparencies have all been for the entire classroom or for larger groups. Perhaps the tape recorder and the eight-millimeter film clips more recently on the market are more useful for individuals and small groups and are thus exceptions to the generality of industries' products being most useful for mass education. But I don't think that industries' new products will be for large groups. Earlier, they were making products for the general public that we were adapting to school purposes. Now they will be making products for us, and they know that our greatest need is to individualize instruction. If the industries are to succeed in the education market, and they seldom fail, they will produce programs and materials that will lend themselves to the teaching of individuals, not classrooms or schools. It may tax your imagination to visualize having on hand just the right kind of early diagnosis, just the right introductory materials, just the right practice materials, just the right applications of the skills and just the right evaluation devices for each child, but this is what the new technology must provide to be successful, and I think that it will come. When it does come, teachers will be better able to assume the role that they always should have had—that of diagnostician and therapist (in the medical rather than the psychological sense) for individual children.

If teachers work together in this new scheme of things, and I would hope that they would, their cooperation would be toward better understanding of individual children and their needs, rather than in separate roles for mass and small-group instruction that we now know as team teaching. The team, if there is one, would involve the sharing of ideas about how the communications skills are shaping up for an individual student. It would amount to a consultation or a clinical approach to a case study toward better diagnosis and prescription.

If I have been hard on mass education it may be because I believe that there is some truth in the observation that it is "intellectual crop dusting." We may resent the mass bombardment of such a communications medium as TV, and we might even wish that children did not spend so much time with it, but we would be naive indeed if we didn't recognize it as a social reality that changes patterns of communication.

Dr. Wilbur Schramm of the Stanford Institute for Communications Research reports a study dealing with the vocabulary development of children in a TV community and a non-TV community. I found it interesting that Wilbur Schramm found it necessary to go to western Canada to find a non-TV community. At any rate he found that in the preschool years, television is a very important learning source. Both bright children and slow children who have been exposed to television, the study concludes, start school with vocabularies about a grade higher than those children who have been without the benefit of television. Similarly, children of average intelligence who are heavy viewers start school with greater vocabularies than those of children who are light viewers.[2] It would seem then that our kindergarten and primary programs ought to take advantage of these TV developed vocabularies. Did you ever consider how easy it would be to teach children to read if we were to develop our pre-primer and primer stories about beer, cigarettes, cosmetics and soap? I'm not advocating that, but reading readiness would be no problem.

Another recent curriculum development is the movement toward the nongraded school. You probably recognize this as one that began in the primary grades, as did many other curriculum innovations, and was usually and sometimes solely concerned with the teaching of reading. John Goodlad and Robert Anderson pushed hard for adoption of the nongraded concept throughout the elementary school, and Frank Brown has publicized the nongraded high school at Melbourne, Florida.

In its early stages, the nongraded primary involved only two things—an acceptance of the idea of continuous promotion for the first four years of schooling (K-3) and an extension of the number of attainment levels in beginning reading from four to about twenty. This was a good beginning step. Goodlad and others had earlier laid a sound research basis for the practice of continuous promotion, and the idea of multi-leveling the first four years of reading instruction called attention to the individual differences that were always there. There were, however, several weaknesses in this plan. Almost without exception the content of these programs was constant and the time variable. In other words it was simply a repackaging of the same old stuff under the assumption that all children should learn the same thing, but at different rates. The fallacy of this assumption is obvious. Children who differ widely in abilities, needs and interests should have different content, different materials and different methods.

Another major fallacy of the nongraded primary concept was that there was no sensible rationale for ending this program at the end of grade three. What do you do with the child who completes all the steps in three rather than four years? If the idea makes sense, it makes just as much sense in grades four, five, and six and in the junior and senior high school as it does in the kindergarten and first three grades. The concept of continuous promotion will hold up for all grades; why not make the entire school nongraded?

Then again, what is so special about reading to make it the one and only basis for multi-leveling instruction? Why not do it also in writing, speaking and listening? Why not in mathematics, the social studies and science? The aim is, and should always have been, to individualize instruction in all subjects at all levels. Multi-leveling is one step toward this goal.

A recent check on the research on the nongraded school finds substantial evidence on both sides. I found fourteen studies completed during the past seven years comparing nongraded and graded schools. Nine of these favored the nongraded programs. Four favored the graded programs and one found no difference. Seven of the fourteen studies were doctoral dissertations. Four favored nongrading and three opposed it. I imagine that they all got their degrees, but it probably is safe to say that the question is still at issue.

It is interesting to note that Robert Carbone, investigator in one of the studies where the results did not favor the nongraded school, observed that the teachers in the nongraded schools he researched appeared to operate much the same as the teachers in the graded schools used as a control. The point needs to be made that the nongraded plan is a system of organization and nothing more. Unless the methods and materials change to take advantage of the potential of the new organization, there is likely to be no advantage to it.

If the effects of the industrial revolution in education that I predicted earlier become a reality and focus upon individualized instruction, it is not difficult to foresee that all of the content subjects, and surely those involving the communications skills, will be nongraded at all levels. Multi-leveling is a trend in keeping with the most basic goals in methodology and is sure to continue.

We have talked here about current curriculum developments related to the communications skills, especially developments in the reselection of content in terms of the structure of subjects, care for deviant portions of the population, psychological aspects of communication, the technological revolution on the horizon, and nongradedness. Each of these has affected and is affecting instruction in the skills of communication. In closing, let me remind you that these developments exert more change upon the way we do things than upon what we are trying to do. Teaching is constant diagnosis and prescription and to do these well means prescribing for *individuals.* Our methods with the skills of communication will be good to the extent that they encourage this diagnosis and to the extent that they enable us to carry out the prescription.

1. Jerome S. Bruner, *The Process of Education* (Cambridge: Harvard University Press, 1961), p. 7.

2. Wilbur Schramm, Jack Lyle, and Edwin B. Parker, *Television in the Lives of Our Children,* (Stanford, California: Stanford University Press, 1961), pp. 75-97.

# The Role of the Teacher

Part Four

*Literacy is not the mere mastery of language, but a mastery of those areas of experience which it communicates. Language is the signal and the product of thought, and the province of literacy is virtually the entire province of the human mind.*

# Literature and Literacy

## by Edward W. Rosenheim, Jr.

There is one experience which English teachers encounter over and over again and which almost always takes the same form. You meet someone for the first time and, in due course, you let fall the fact that, for better or for worse, you teach English. "Oh," exclaims the new-found friend, "I'd better watch my grammar." At this point the English teacher's reaction becomes highly individualized, and each of us adopts his own strategy: the disparaging simper, the patient explanation, the outright flight, the pithy epithet, even, perhaps, the act of violence. The choice is up to the individual and I (who happen to go in for an abrupt change of subject) scruple to prescribe for anyone else.

But I am not going to dismiss the phenomenon. Instead, as an experience familiar to all teachers of English, it will form the

Dr. Edward W. Rosenheim, Jr.
Professor of English
Department of English
University of Chicago

starting point for this precarious attempt of mine to discuss some problems which I think are as general and as real as—and infinitely more important than—the trivial encounter itself. I'm going to suggest that we consider this threadbare cliche, not as evidence of the speaker's ignorance or banality, but as evidence of his opinion as to what English teachers are supposed to do. In other words, precisely because we hear this kind of thing so often, I think we may take it seriously as an indication of the *role* which is generally assigned to our profession.

The role, as the words "I'd better watch . . ." suggest, is in part the role of the stereotypical schoolmaster; in the presence of *any* teacher, that is, each of us, however adult, had "better watch" something or other. Actually, I suspect, our new-found friend has probably used "grammar" as a shorthand statement for other things as well. It is very likely that "I'd better watch my grammar" means, "To the extent that this English teacher can inspect them, I'd better watch my grammar *and* my choice of words, and perhaps I'd better try to sound 'intelligent' about the things I've read and the plays I've seen."

In effect, we English teachers have been widely viewed as the custodians of an orthodoxy—the proprietors and practitioners of a set of systems, by which we are not only able to teach people reading and writing but to assess the degree to which they have succeeded and to prescribe firmly how they ought to write and what they ought to read. This is what I have referred to as our "role"; it is a set of general expectations growing up around an image or an ideal of the English teacher. As such, of course, these expectations are rarely, if ever, entirely fulfilled when one encounters a particular English teacher—any more than the classical role of president of the United States or friendly family physician or policeman or mother or father is entirely fulfilled on our examination of individual specimens. But the role mysteriously survives many such disappointments. Moreover, as recent studies have suggested, we are only beginning to ask the most interesting questions about a role when we ask whether it has been played in a way that satisfies other people. The more difficult, but equally significant, questions have to do with the effect of the role upon *oneself*, the player of it—the function of the role in dictating our own standards and expectations, in producing and sometimes resolving our own conflicts, in providing for each of us his own frustrations and satisfactions.

I have spoken of the role of the English teacher as that of custodian and practitioner of what I've so far only defined as an orthodoxy—a set of systems by which the arts of linguistic communication can be cultivated, judged, and made permanent.

When I seek for a single term to describe the object of our preservation and practice, I can come up with no better word than "literacy." Literacy has been, in fact, a rather comforting concept, in both its orthodoxy and its flexibility. As an orthodoxy, it has provided us with a tailor-made standard by which we can judge between the elect and the unregenerate, even determining in some jurisdictions those who can and cannot have a voice in the conduct of our political destiny, those who can and cannot hold various jobs, those who can and cannot be regarded as responsible adults. It can be applied with similar assurance to define the stages of the educational process (a normal, unpushed first grader ought to be illiterate; a third grader darn well better not be); to qualify the foreigner for citizenship in the republic; to "improve" the holders of menial, poorly paid jobs so that they qualify for better ones. Literacy, in such instances, can be a sharp, sure instrument of discrimination (for better or worse), and the difference between the literate and illiterate emerges as one of kind rather than degree.

On the other hand, the concept of literacy can also take on a very handy flexibility. We are able, in many cases, to talk about the more and the less literate person, to damn with the term "illiterate" those whom we regard as barbarous or graceless or just plain stupid, even though they are demonstrably able to read and write. We can speak approvingly of books or plays or conversations as "highly" literate, and we can and do speak of "men of letters" in such a way as to imply that they embody literacy in its highest form. Literacy has, indeed, tended to be equated with such terms as "civilization" or, in the old-fashioned, Matthew Arnold sense, with "culture."

It is reassuring to the English teacher to think that his role is to cultivate and nourish arts which seem so potent. It is also reassuring to think that we English teachers are, if anyone is, the appointed guardians of the monuments of literacy—those poems and plays and novels and other discourses which have been wrought by the art of letters and are, as it were, the permanent products and prizes of literacy. Literacy, it has been argued, achieves its true form and total fulfillment at the point at which it acquires lasting shape—when, ceasing to be mere communication, it becomes the "product of deliberate, artful construction in language, designed to stand in permanent form, with the capacity to bring pleasure or enlightenment or both to those who hear or read it."

Now I'm by no means confident that every English teacher would blandly define his role as that of custodian and propagator of literacy. But I do strongly suspect that some such role is assigned us by the more sympathetic members of our society—

whether they watch their grammar in our presence, or ask our opinions of new books, or, obviously most important, turn over their young to us in the expectation that we can cultivate within them the faculties and habits of literacy.

The concept of literacy I have been describing and the role I have been trying to define have taken a heavy pounding in recent years. And in recent months I have come to feel, with great urgency, that both concept and role are threatened with extinction. Rather than document this impression with abstractions or statistics, let me presume on your friendship with some autobiography.

In August of 1967, my wife and I and two of our sons departed for thirteen months in London. The period of time we spent in England turned out to be, as I saw it, a glorious and almost total immersion in literacy. My days were largely spent at "work" in the British Museum Reading Room—itself perhaps the most massive monument to literacy in the world. I spent a lot of time reading old books, in which the wit and wisdom and devotion as well as the passion and folly and prejudice of the early eighteenth century were permanently and, as a rule, engagingly recorded. I did a certain amount of writing and often found myself fatuously imagining that by some form of osmosis my own prose had acquired a heightened dimension of literacy, engendered by great models and insulation from term papers. We were able to visit the Houses of Parliament and there were exposed to a brand of rhetoric that usually conformed to my highest expectation—complete with learned allusions and Latin tags, timely jests, and an irony that could be delicate or savage as the occasion required. Much of our leisure was spent in those citadels of literacy, the London theaters and the London bookshops. But even more commonplace aspects of our life seemed equally to bear the stamp of literacy. Thanks to BBC, television and radio were saturated with the signals of familiarity with books and with respect for the uses of the English tongue. They seemed to assume our interest in ideas and our discriminating preference for what was serious; even British TV soap opera is produced with imagination and taste, ingeniously scripted, and superlatively acted. The stamp of literacy was apparent on the majority of the Britons themselves—including many whom one would hardly regard as "intellectual." We heard facile and gracious conversation from policemen and shopkeepers. Even the pubs of South London—which we sometimes explored for purely clinical reasons—abounded in that special kind of unpretentious linguistic virtuosity that is the hallmark of cockney slang, cockney wit, cockney irony.

Let us say that I returned to America in September 1968 in a state of starry-eyed euphoria—that I had never felt more keenly the power and appeal and capacity for survival of literacy in its richest sense. And let us note some of the things I discovered as I emerged from my dream:

*Item:* The most widely discussed and fashionable English professor on the North American continent was gleefully predicting, indeed describing, the disappearance of letters, and hence literacy, under the pressures exerted by other media of communication.

*Item:* A single dirty word, written on the forehead of a post-adolescent, was able to elicit, on the spot, more passionate responses than have been evoked by Lincoln's Gettysburg address in the whole of the past century.

*Item:* In universities throughout the land, allegedly literate men and women professed adherence to a "philosophy" which, they triumphantly declared, was concerned neither with principles nor ultimate objectives nor with rational discourse nor with stated doctrines but with "action"—and often militant action—as an end in itself.

*Item:* The television set, in itself a miracle of communication quite as adaptable to the services of literacy as the theater, had become the official arena of non-literacy. Within a form constricted by time segments, station-breaks, Neilsen ratings, and commercial rewards, there flourished a carnival of rhythmic grunts and bleats, shaking torsos, pratfalls, and embraces; of impoverished formulas for unfunny comedy, predictable melodrama, ritualistic horse opera; of fugitive, formless fragments of small talk from "celebrities"; and, of course, of glittering charades, performed to the greater glory of pain-killers, pile-cures, deodorants, and detergents.

*Item:* The theater itself seemed, in large part, systematically determined to detach itself from literacy and to combine verbal, visual, and even physical assault upon the audience in some form of shock treatment. Within a few months of my return, for example, I was privileged to pay five dollars in order to watch a man standing immobile and unspeaking upon a stage for twenty-five minutes as the prelude to a three-hour performance whose literary component consisted of some seventy-five words, chanted in some ten slogans that would have seemed banal to Emma Goldman and Eugene Debs.

*Item:* The Vietnam War, the most profound tragedy of our time, was, by some sort of tacit consent, immune from virtually any discussion—on the air or in print—more penetrating or literate than the pious profession of hope, the stock formulas of dismay, or the frank confession of bewilderment. It was clearly not a subject for sustained thought or discussion but, instead, a TV performance to be watched over a can of beer.

*Item*, item, item . . . to suggest that language itself was being assailed in an effort to destroy the dimension of literacy. A word such as "relevant," once the very signal for an austere insistence on responsible, useful and apposite communication, became the sloppiest possible expression of approval or disapproval. One no longer dares ask, "Relevant to what?" for relevance has become the stock device for evading just this question. The word "radical," traditionally signifying a concern for basic or "root" problems, has become a catchword for those who resolutely disdain an engagement with just such problems. The word "like," after a long, respectable history as both adjective and conjunction, has become a sort of verbal tic-habit, a noise to be inserted, at frequent and random intervals, presumably to signify that the speaker is, like, resentful at having to speak at all.

But by now I hope you recognize that what I have been saying is less than just. We all know that British literacy is, to a considerable extent, illusory and that it is accompanied by some staggering ineptitude in the conduct of public affairs. We know as well that Britain continues to suffer from species of material and educational privation which turn the urbane eloquence of its leaders into a kind of nasty mockery. More important, we know that not all the American phenomena I have mentioned are peculiarly American, nor do they rise exclusively from folly or caprice or greed. Often they reflect a considered rejection of received values, an honest disdain for rules of the game that have been found wanting in the grim arena of contemporary life. As such, they can be viewed as symbols of dissatisfaction with a culture that has bred disgraceful inequities and areas of profound and authentic need.

I have given this slanted account of my own experience because it offers a paradigm—or, if you will, a parable or a caricature—of the English teacher, cherishing his traditional role, clutching his traditional self-image, when confronted with stern actualities that threaten role and image with extinction. And these actualities, however they may threaten our professional identity, are by no means exclusively destructive.

When problems are acute and immediate, our responses tend to take extreme form. Our own profession's responses to the threats I have been describing have, in many instances, pursued one of two opposed extremes, neither of which seems very attractive to me. On the one hand, there is what might be described as the armed-fortress reaction. Those who adopt it seem determined to preserve unchanged the received tradition of literacy, protecting it, whole and unsullied, from the assaults of the barbarians. Here the self-image tends to be that of a small but resolute band, a literate elite, prepared to lock itself and its treasure within a stronghold that can resist all encroachments. Here there is a resolute determination to preserve intact the values, the works, the rules which comprise the cherished ortho-doxy—or perhaps only to preserve the starry-eyed vision of tweedy urbanity to which I succumbed in England. But the line to be held is clear. Great books remain immutably great. The rules of spelling, grammar, and syntax, the canons of "good" writing, the principles of literary decorum—these comprise the sacred tradition. It is a tradition that can be eloquently defended with phrases about the timelessness of truth, aphorisms about ancient messages for today's youth, and the pious belief that, though firmly locked within their citadel, the elect can somehow, some day, magically effect the conversion of the infidel.

This position is not merely ridiculous; it is inhumane and immoral. It implies that whatever love we are capable of should be lavished on a tradition rather than our fellow man. It blinds us to the fact that the barbarian hordes are not our enemy; they are our fellow citizens, our students, our own children. They may be unlovable, aggressive, even violent; the temptation to counter their assaults with disdain and rejection is often enor-mously powerful. But to yield to this temptation, to retreat into contemptuous isolation, is, in effect, utterly to abandon our role as citizens and especially as teachers.

At the opposite extreme from the armed-fortress response is the course of abdication, of confusion and flight—however subtly and respectably the flight may be disguised as some form of "progress." We can, that is, abandon our role as custodians of literacy but, unlike the denizens of the armed fortress, we can proclaim our continuing usefulness as teachers. We shall not, to be sure, be teachers of letters but of something else such as anthropology or social problems or communications.

The pressures on many of us to do these things are very real and powerful. It has been accurately remarked that today's schools are far more than educational establishments; they are frequently the most important social agency in the community, affording every service from physical nourishment to psycho-therapy, from group recreation to family counseling, from medical care to police protection. As you all know, there are universities which today serve social purposes that twenty years ago would have been totally alien to their function—and there is every reason to feel that if these institutions expect continuing public and private support, their functions must increasingly pro-liferate. A large, private, urban university, such as my own, faces heavy responsibilities as landlord and urban planner, as clinic for a huge range of physical, emotional, and social disorders, as supplier of political advice and leadership, as a center for research and consultation, much of which must be immediately responsive to public need.

Inevitably—although many of us lament the fact—the definition of a university has changed within the minds of many students and parents and members of the general population. For these people, a university is no longer a searcher and communicator of knowledge; it is, variously, a participatory democracy, an arena for political warfare, a conspiratorial ally of Big Business, a vital branch of Big Government, an amorphous "service agency" whose activities and products are flexibly determined by the needs of particular segments of society at particular moments. Such definitions are produced both by the university's friends and by its enemies, but in either case, whether we concur in them or resist them, they are singularly hard to reconcile with our traditional identity and our traditional dedication.

It is little wonder that today the role, and hence the day-to-day career, of the English teacher is constantly subject to profound change. It is little wonder that, while there is ever more talk about "communication," there is ever less talk about *composition,* about clarity or grace or logic or consistency. It is not surprising that in our councils and committees there are constantly diminishing opportunities to concern ourselves with letters and literature and constantly increasing pressures to concern ourselves with political strategies. Nor is it surprising that the classroom itself shares these pressures and is likely to become the arena of talk about "student problems" or that the teacher finds himself thrust ever more often into the role of antagonist or mediator, psychologist, apologist, organizer, guide, philosopher, friend—anything and everything but the custodian and cultivator of literacy. And finally, it is not strange that in these circumstances the monuments of literacy, Homer and Shakespeare and Dante and Milton, and indeed the concern for the past itself move farther and farther into the background.

The conscientious English teacher may desperately seek accommodation. He may, if he is so inclined, discover that the Living Theater or the movies of Andy Warhol or the poetry of the poetic Beatle or the polemics of Herbert Marcuse somehow bridge, however shakily, the gap between the tradition and the immediate actuality. He may yield helplessly to the demands, capricious and unexamined as they may be, of "relevance," which—while they may proceed from anything, from real social concern to utter whimsicality—are not likely to lead to much of relevance to the teaching of English. He may alter not only the substance but the basic principles of what he teaches so as to meet the character of today's mass media or the gnawing demands for attention and self-esteem presented by his students.

Today there are college English courses totally devoted to a handful of fifth-rate books because they are claimed to be "relevant" by students who have never read them—or much else. There are other courses devoted to "problems" and "issues" in which literature serves merely as the momentary spring-board for elaborate and inconclusive bull sessions. There are teachers everywhere and at every level for whom the microphone and film-strip and tape recorder have superseded—not, as they importantly can, augmented—the written word. And there are, tragically, teachers who simply do not teach—because confrontations and rebuffs and frustrations have turned them from teachers into victims, expert only in the arts of negotiation or evasion or in a sullen travesty of the gestures of teaching.

It is probably true that many teachers other than those of English are confronted with the circumstances I have been describing. But I believe the English teacher suffers a special vulnerability. For the basic fabric of his calling is being assailed, not only by the hostile forces of dissent and disorder, but by, as it were, the benevolent competition of new modes of inquiry and communication. Between them, hostility and competition provide a combination so formidable that even the extreme forms of abdication I have mentioned are not hard to understand.

When a man discusses extremes, he is usually setting things up to plead for a middle ground, and these remarks of mine are no exception. Certainly, today a monolithic conception of literacy is indefensible—and I imagine it always has been. Literacy is surely doomed if it is exclusively defined either as a mere tool to be turned to unspecified purposes or as the mastery of an inert mass of information and principles and practices. For the simple fact—so simple that many of us forget it—is that the power and nobility and permanence and complexity of language are derived directly from the presence of those qualities in the concepts and imaginings and actualities which language is used to communicate. Literacy is not the mere mastery of language, but a mastery of those areas of experience which it communicates. Language is the signal and the product of thought, and the province of literacy is virtually the entire province of the human mind.

Today's world poses a threat to literacy in some measure because of the militancy, suspicion, and intellectual irresponsibility which disdain letters as well as much else that is humane. But in at least equal measure the challenge arises because of so much that is new, because of what Robert Oppenheimer somewhere called "the prevalence of novelty," because, in short, there is so much to be literate *about*. If we are to be accepted as custodians and purveyors of literacy, it is not because we are watching someone's grammar. We shall continue to be accepted only because there is confidence in our curiosity and alertness to what is being asked and learned about the world and society and the human personality. And we shall be expected, moreover, to seek an orderly understanding of much that is disorderly, of much that is unlovely and confusing, but which, because it is real and immediate, demands to be understood.

Between the extremes of the armed fortress and the various forms of surrender, therefore, there lies the literacy whose allegiance is to unflagging curiosity, whose sign of triumph is understanding, whose real enemies are ignorance and those habits of mind by which ignorance is enthroned. We may call this the literacy of the middle road, but, unlike some middle roads, it is a path to be taken only by the courageous and inquiring soul—willing to relinquish safe shibboleths and comfortable parochialisms, but unwilling to take counsel of those who are the manifest foes, I will not say of truth itself, but of the quest for truth.

I have thus far talked chiefly about literacy and have said little about literature. And frankly, as you must know, teachers in a university do not very often talk about literacy but about books. The "researches" of most of my colleagues, that is, are directed to a better understanding of books; they are variously engaged in restoring and preserving and interpreting and assessing what I have called the monuments of literacy. It is very easy to make this kind of undertaking, like many other kinds of research, appear hopelessly remote from the actualities that most immediately concern us all. I need not remind you of the caricatures or maliciously chosen examples which can be used to show how idle and inconsequential such activities can be. Yet I believe that an understanding of the *products* of literacy is crucial in our response to the inescapable problems which we all confront at this hour.

For it seems to me that, at every level, literacy involves creation—an affirmative act of the understanding in which letters, themselves lifeless, are forged into the living word. In this sense, the act of *re*-creation which the beginning reader in the first grade undertakes is genuinely creative, and so, of course, are his first scrawled words on the page. In both cases, from mere latent symbols, he has "made something"; he has made his name or a statement or a little story—or he has, simply, "made sense" of materials from which sense was previously lacking. The creation and the creative understanding of those works we somewhat arbitrarily call literature or even "great" literature involve the same kind of act. The difference is one of degree, although an obviously great degree. To the extent that a literary work is imaginative, complex, emotionally invested, intellectually provocative, to the same extent will our qualities of intellect, imagination, and spirit emerge in a successful encounter with it. When today we ask for "constructive" discourse, we ask for the abandonment of mere gesture, physical or verbal, which signifies only passion and invites nothing save passion from us. We ask, indeed, for literate construction, for the *making* of a fabric of thought, to which we can respond with an affirmative, equally creative act of understanding.

It is the reluctance to create and to honor the products of creation that is most terrifying about the various manifestations of pure militancy, that is most depressing about the threadbare rituals of the mass media or the low-level McCluhanism which views men as passive receptors and helpless victims of technological change. When literacy is abandoned we all become victims, for to gestures that are nothing more than the unshaped expression of raw feeling—the gestures of illiteracy—one is fatally tempted to respond with equally mindless hatred or contempt. In neither gesture nor response is there the hint of a work of the mind. In such "confrontation"—whether it masquerades as art or as "dialogue"—there is only rejection of man's unique capacity for intellectual creation. And, on the other hand, the act of rational discourse is an act of creation, of art. Creation of this kind is the characteristic and redeeming activity of the academic community in its most truly humane aspect.

Teachers of English should be talking about everything under the sun—for the province of literacy is no more limited than that. Yet our conversation, like our work, cannot be idle or random or uncritical. It can achieve order and rigor and usefulness if it is indeed a creation, a "making," a shaping of comprehension and imagination and feeling into a unity which has not existed before. For us, as for the artist, the will and ability to create are capable of forging, from the very tumult and dissatisfaction which surround us today, the affirmative plans and doctrines—the works of the mind—that are our only salvation.

In *The Eighth Day*, a new novel by Thornton Wilder, I discovered two sentences that express the most fundamental thing I believe about our role today. They represent the kind of thing that one teacher can say most profitably and hearteningly to another:

"There is no creation without faith and hope. There is no faith and hope that does not express itself in creation." [1]

1. Thornton Wilder, *The Eighth Day* (New York: Harper & Row, Publishers, 1967), p. 107. Reprinted by permission of the publisher.

*The new key word is* engagement. *But this concern, excitement, involvement, engagement must lead to a restructuring of the inner self. As a result of his experience, the student develops a better understanding of himself; he has a clearer, deeper insight into the human condition; there are more options in his responses to life, and these responses become more creative. In short, he is more humane.*

# The Floating Curriculum

## by Robert A. Bennett

The floating curriculum presents an image, that of a voyage from home port to destination, from birth to full mastery and control of language, or for our purposes, that portion of the voyage which takes us through the various concerns of the English curriculum. We plan a smooth, "articulated" trip to calm the wind and waves of artificial grade level and course designations. But above all, we must be on course; we dare not drift. Our goal must be clear, and our measurements of our progress toward that goal must be precise.

Before we embark on our voyage with the floating curriculum today, we must consider our special role. We want smooth sail-

**Dr. Robert A. Bennett**
Specialist, Language Arts
San Diego Unified School District
San Diego, California

ing for our students, yet our goal cannot be achieved just by "floating down the river on a lazy Sunday afternoon." Administrators and teachers must see that where the action is, there is the student. One superintendent defined our role this way. "We hire administrators whose function is to take command of a smooth steady ship, but we also have supervisors who keep rocking the boat as much as they can."

The journey from kindergarten to graduation is a long one, with at least four important ports of call—reading, language, composition, and literature. The function of the crew, the teachers and administrative officials, will depend, in part, on how we are organized. Here is an example from one large school system—San Diego.

In this unified district with about 170,000 students in the kindergarten through the junior college program, curriculum leadership in the English language arts is under the direction of a specialist. Working with him on the curriculum team are two instructional consultants on the elementary level (one who specializes in reading and one in the other areas of the program) and three instructional consultants at the secondary level (one in reading, one in speech and drama, and one in English). In addition there is a team of district resource teachers selected from among the most capable classroom teachers in the district to work from the central office for a period of three years. At the site level are in-school resource teachers in elementary schools, demonstration teachers in both elementary and secondary schools, and department chairmen in secondary schools and junior colleges. All are regular classroom teachers who are given, depending on their assignment, additive pay, substitute service, teacher aides, and/or reduced teaching loads.

The resource staff works with an independent testing department, which is responsible for reporting program evaluation to the superintendent and the Board of Education. This staff selects and creates instruments to measure growth toward the objectives of the curriculum. As a result of this evaluation, teams of teachers, working with the resource staff, plan needed curriculum revisions and evaluate new instructional materials. Individual teachers are employed on an hourly basis during the school year or during the summer to implement the recommendations of these committees through the preparation of curriculum guides. These guides are designed to free the individual classroom teacher from the overwhelming task of planning an articulated program from grade to grade and course to course and to provide a common statement of goals, many illustrations of teaching strategies to reach these goals, and evaluation procedures to measure student progress. The teacher uses the guide to plan the most appropriate program of instruction for each student assigned to him.

All new curriculum programs and instructional materials are submitted to a Curriculum Council for recommendation to the superintendent and through him to the Board of Education. This council comprises specialists from all subject areas and representatives from the operating divisions of the district. Its function is to provide a balanced program of instruction for all students in the district.

The process of curriculum development typically follows these ten steps:

(1) Evaluation of ongoing programs in the district
(2) Reassessment and formulation of basic goals of instruction
(3) Study of programs developed by federally funded projects, by national professional associations, by the state department of education, and by other school districts
(4) Attack on the problems and issues best solved by local study and experimentation
(5) Identification of content, skills, and attitudes essential for achievement of goals
(6) Planning the sequence of instruction and identifying the most effective teaching strategies
(7) Selection of instructional materials
(8) Preparation of curriculum guides
(9) Orientation of all teachers using these guides
(10) Evaluation of the program in the classroom and modification of the guides based on this experience.

In addition to curriculum development, the second main function of the resource team is to provide leadership for the in-service education program. The most important single factor in its success will be the establishment of a professional climate in which teachers, administrators, and resource personnel will freely recognize both their individual strengths and their weaknesses in their professional backgrounds and competencies. No one is expert in all phases of such a complex field; each can develop his unique strengths; all need periodic updating. There are many ways of providing professional growth opportunities. Here are a few we have found most effective:

(1) Participation in curriculum development
(2) District-sponsored college credit courses
(3) City-wide and departmental meetings
(4) Educational television directed at teachers and at students
(5) Demonstration lessons

(6) Demonstration schools
(7) Workshops and seminars sponsored by publishers
(8) Use of community resources such as professional authors and technical writers
(9) Professional organizations and conferences.

It is a function of the local resource staff to provide an atmosphere of relevancy by relating this in-service program to current curriculum development objectives. Leadership personnel must play an active role by assessing the needs of the program as well as the strengths and weaknesses of the teaching staff, by designing appropriate opportunities, by counseling with individual teachers, and by participating fully in the program as they recognize as curriculum leaders their own needs for professional growth and demonstrate by their own actions the value of these experiences.

As we launch the floating curriculum and head toward our first port of call, each member of the crew has his assigned duties:

(1) the teacher to grow professionally by participating in curriculum development and in-service education opportunities and as a result to improve his instructional program by using his classroom as a laboratory;
(2) the in-school resource teacher and the English department chairman of each building to participate in district projects, to adapt district and/or state programs to the unique needs of a particular student body, and to work cooperatively with teachers in other departments in helping them achieve their goals and in soliciting their help in achieving the goals of the English program;
(3) the district resource personnel to provide leadership in planning, to participate as a learning member of the team, and to communicate ideas and needs to district administrators and through them to the Board of Education; and finally
(4) the Board of Education to communicate through district administrators the general goals of the educational program, to have faith in the professional staff to implement these goals, and to provide this staff with the resources needed to build the strongest possible educational program.

## Reading

There is no single approach that can reach across the range of skills needed for effective reading, beginning with decoding printed letters into their corresponding language sounds and moving through comprehension and application of what is read to complex thought processes. Individuals learn best by different methods. Each skill is best taught by a unique strategy. Clearly the need is for a broad, eclectic, multi-dimensional program.

Research has much to say about the teaching of reading. The Denver studies demonstrate the importance of beginning instruction in the kindergarten and, if this is to have a positive effect, of modifying the traditional program in the elementary grades. Jeanne Chall's *Learning to Read:* The Great Debate provides evidence of the need for early emphasis on developing code breaking skills as opposed to lengthy story line explications of selections without story lines.[1] The U.S. Office of Education's "First and Second Grade Reading Study" concludes that the greatest factor in the success of a reading program is the teacher —I doubt if it's the color of her eyes, the style of her hair, the length of her mini-skirt, or even the nature of her personality. I suggest, rather, that it's the effectiveness of her teaching methods, not just the materials she uses.

New materials are abundantly available from publishers. We've progressed from the early color-me-brown texts to imaginative series that honestly reflect the experiences of children from many of the cultural and ethnic backgrounds found in the mosaic we call America. It is important for all children to discover a reflection of themselves in the books they read, but it is equally important for all children to understand those book characters whom they have not yet had an opportunity to know.

Many opportunities must be provided to practice the code breaking skills independently (without the teacher preteaching every new word), to read for sustained periods of time and to organize materials from various sources, to develop those unique skills needed in various content areas, to develop the ability to use reference materials, and to interpret and apply what is read. And these experiences must be continued through the grades to high school graduation and beyond.

Some of the most effective high school programs use the technique of an all-department reading committee. Interested teachers from each subject area sponsor displays of books (especially paperbacks) and encourage wide reading in their areas of instruction. They know that the key to a successful program is to provide material on a wide range of difficulty levels to match the maturity and interests of their students. They also realize the need to provide an instructional framework for the basic text provided their students and ask such questions as: What assumptions does the author make about the background of the reader? What is his style for presenting facts, supporting evidence, and generalizations? What is the text's organizational pattern and how are such typographical devices as italics and headings used to help the reader understand this organization? How can I help students to discover relationships among concepts, to identify major ideas from their support, to separate facts from opinions, to detect inferences, and to apply the knowledge gained?

Individuals are often lost in a study of the averages, means, and medians of test data. There is no magic program in which all achieve the goals we have set. Early reading-disability prevention programs and some form of continuous progress instruction beginning in primary grades are required. Summer diagnostic clinics, reading centers, and high school reading laboratories are all essential extensions of the classroom teacher if each student is to have his equal opportunity for a successful voyage on the floating curriculum.

## Language

First, it is a creation of man, and as such, it is his greatest achievement, one that sets him apart from all other forms of life. Every major advance in the history of civilization has been made possible only because man has invented a reliable system of communication. But as an invention of man, it is subject to changes as man changes, and it also has as many varieties as men are different from each other from culture to culture, from young to old, and from individual to individual. Man's language is primarily oral; writing is a variety of language that only partially represents the spoken word with its limited capacity for indicating stress, pitch, and juncture.

Language represents man's observation of his environment, and because his universe is infinitely intricate, his language is equally complex. Through language man is able not only to communicate his reaction to the here and now (as can other animals), but also his reflections of the past and his dreams of the future. Thus language is distinctly human, and through language each man develops his core of selfhood. It is a deeply personal possession; to attack my language is to attack my inner self.

Finally, we know that language is learned. Although the baby is born with the capacity to master a portion of its complexities, growth in language power is a lifelong pursuit. Pediatricians claim they can differentiate within weeks of birth the baby who frequently hears the sounds of the human voice from the infant who does not, from the quality and nature of his babblings. Thus the first step in language learning is through imitation. The paucity of early oral-aural experiences of a child before he enters school is the major source of the problem of disadvantaged youth. During this period of greatest growth in language mastery, the child learns to imitate the phonemic, morphemic, and syntactic sounds and patterns of his dialect. Sometimes differences between his dialect and the dialect of the larger society he may enter later will be rewarded, but more often the differences will result in social and economic punishment. Here the concept of a dual dialect is important. The goal of second dialect learning is not to replace a home language with a school language, but rather to add to the linguistic capability of the child the ability to move from one to the other. Walter Loban's studies, among others, have demonstrated the child's need to maintain the dialect he brings to school for his self-pride, for his continued communication in the home, and for his survival on the street.

The process of language learning, of course, does not end with imitation. Children come to school creating new sentences. Through generalization and internalization, the child enters school as a living, talking, grammatical being.

*The grammar* exists in the mind of a native speaker of a language. His brain is like a computer, and the process of language learning involves the connecting of response wires. The number of linguistic choices he must make every minute he speaks is phenomenal. Grammars, on the other hand, are attempts to explain this internalized behavior. None will ever be complete. Language study within the school program aims to provide insight into a distinctly human activity.

Language is much broader than just the study of grammar. It has an important history that will help our students appreciate its beauty and complexity. Exploration of semantics will reveal the power of language as symbol and code. Also, a knowledge of usage patterns, regional and cultural dialects, functional varieties, and appropriate linguistic choices is essential for success and often for survival in our multi-cultural society.

Although there is much that must be taught through careful instruction, discovery is a much more interesting and effective way to explore some of the mysteries of language. In many ways the teacher can serve as simply a guide whose object is to keep the students headed in the right direction. Exploration of language is never completed. Much experience with language is vital to our enjoyment and success in reading, composition, and literature.

## Composition

Composition is like Siamese twins, separated in places, but growing together in others. One is called written composition; the other, oral composition. Students need time to talk as they develop their capacity to use words to deal with inner and outer experience. Through an oral rehearsal of ideas in which they receive reactions to those ideas from their peers and have opportunities to modify and add to their own store of ideas from listening to others, our students will be better prepared for their experiences in written composition. Student-centered oral discussion has long been our major mode of oral composition. The Dartmouth Seminar papers suggested innovative and more exciting methods. Improvisation, dialogue, and drama are emerging as effective strategies of exploration.

Our experiences in oral composition are essential to success in written composition. There are, however, some different concepts to master in written composition; the rhetoric has some significant differences from its twin that must be understood by our students.

We are concerned primarily with the questions our students ask of themselves as they set out to explore composition. Who am I as an individual? How do I want my "voice" to sound? What resources of language can I use to create this tone? Is there a need for me to inform, convince, persuade, stimulate, entertain, or convey a feeling, mood, or reflection? To whom am I speaking? What do they know, feel, or believe? What do I think they need to know, feel, or believe?

Education is concerned with the organization of inner experience. The child must come to terms with experience before he can symbolize that experience in language. We must focus upon helping the student to discover, interpret, and give form to his ideas about human experience. It begins with the stimulation of thought—his thoughts. As teachers we cannot make discoveries for our students, but we can ask questions that will assist them in reaching these goals. Our questions will help students become aware of the linguistic choices available to them and develop a sensitivity to the effect on their audience of each choice.

We also have another responsibility as teachers. The climate must be just right for the exploration. The only acceptable climate is one in which a student's ideas are accepted as an expression of his thoughts and as important because he is important. Not only his teacher, but also his fellow students must create this atmosphere. And he, as a speaker who is concerned about his audience, must be equally accepting of their reactions, opinions, and honestly stated constructive evaluations. This cooperative atmosphere must be present the year round.

## Literature

To judge by the actions of most English teachers, especially those responsible for secondary education, this is the most important area in the English curriculum, the one to which they like to devote most of their time.

Some of us are concerned that our students develop a knowledge about literature—great authors and their works and sources of the literary idea and allusions from mythology, the *Bible*, and Shakespeare. We want them to develop some sense of literary history. But as William Stafford points out in *Friends to This Ground*, ". . . Man becomes dissatisfied with assuming his ideas to be derived from a reservoir. . . . The values of literature are more and more identified as characteristic of a fountain. . . ." [2]

Others of us are more concerned with helping students develop skill in close reading. We approach literature through its different genres and emphasize plot and character development, use of atmosphere, irony, and symbols, and the relationship of all these to theme.

As important as these considerations may be, more and more of us are recognizing that these approaches are really not worthwhile if our students have not become truly involved (psychologically as well as intellectually) with what they read. They must be concerned over the fate of the characters, and they must become excited over the themes and ideas generated from this experience. The new key word is *engagement*. But this concern, excitement, involvement, engagement must lead to a restructuring of the inner self. As a result of his experience, the student develops a better understanding of himself; he has a clearer, deeper insight into the human condition; there are more options in his responses to life, and these responses become more creative. In short, he is more humane.

Unfortunately, none of these goals can be achieved by merely pushing and forcing our students into reading experiences. Complex and difficult teaching strategies are required. Talk—conversations about literature among students with, at times, the teacher participating as a member of the group—and drama—improvisation, dialogue, and role playing as described by Douglas Barnes in the Dartmouth Seminar papers—are two such methods.

John Gerber in the February 1967 issue of *College English* looked forward to a new period of synthesis of those methods which emphasize detachment, close reading and textual analysis, with those methods which emphasize engagement.[3] This synthesis may be brought about through increased attention to modes and archetypes in literature. Both analysis and engagement are essential for their study.

Certainly we must recognize that it is the literary experience with which we are concerned. This experience was born in an oral tradition, has passed through a print culture, and is now entering an electronic age. The literary experience is available through the ears as well as through the eyes, through movement and action as well as through reading, and through recordings, motion pictures, and television as well as through magazines and books. The literary experience, as Dwight Burton has stated,

> . . . enables the reader to build a level of imaginative living which is very real in itself and which lies somewhere between dead-level literalness and hallucination. Even in so-called escape reading, for example, one comes to terms with experience at the same time that he is escaping from it.[4]

This linking of the inner and outer life is, I think, the essential thing to do.

We come to the end of our cruise on the floating curriculum after visiting briefly the ports of reading, language, composition, and literature. As in all analogies, we have failed to describe reality as it really is. Our ports of call are not isolated cities we can visit one by one. Together, with other ports left unmentioned, they comprise the complex discipline we call English, a discipline which defies attempts to fragment its basic unity.

1. Jeanne Chall, *Learning to Read:* The Great Debate (New York: Mc-Graw-Hill Book Company, 1967).

2. William Stafford, *Friends to This Ground* (Urbana: National Council of Teachers of English, 1968), pp. 2 and 8.

3. John Gerber, "Literature—Our Untamable Discipline," *College English,* Vol. 28 (February 1967), pp. 351-358.

4. Dwight L. Burton, "The Centrality of Literature in the English Curriculum" in *The Range of English,* NCTE Distinguished Lectures of 1968 (Urbana, Illinois: The National Council of Teachers of English, 1968), p. 63.

*. . . supervisors must focus on the few activities which affect each English teacher every week in almost every class.*

# Information Retrieval and the Changing Curriculum

## by Michael F. Shugrue

How little we really know about ourselves as teachers of English! Before the English teacher can understand new theories, assimilate new bodies of knowledge, and employ new classroom techniques, he must first understand what his English classroom is currently like. As a secondary teacher he may not be surprised to learn that literature is emphasized in his classroom teaching 52.2% of the time, composition and language only 15.4% and 13.5% respectively. It will not startle even the good secondary teacher to be told that the mass media are emphasized only 1.3% of the time. Even when he is aware of the emphases in his curriculum, however, he is often woefully unaware of the classroom techniques he employs from day to day.

James R. Squire's *Study of English Programs in Selected High Schools Which Consistently Educate Outstanding Students in English* is valuable not only for its information about the secondary school curriculum but for the myopia about our classroom presentation which it reveals. Squire and his teams of observers

Dr. Michael F. Shugrue
Secretary for English
Modern Language Association of America

asked teachers in 158 schools what methods they most often used in classroom teaching and must have been gratified to learn—from the teachers themselves—that discussion led with 53.6%, that true Socratic questioning occupied 17.6% of classroom time and that lecturing occupied only 14.2% and recitation only 7.0%. What they learned from their own observations, however, was rather different: recitation led with 22.2% of the time, followed closely by lecturing (21.1%) and discussion (19.5%). Socratic questioning, on the other hand, appeared not 17.6% of the time but only 2.2%. Even the good teacher was not capable of leading an examined professional life. In Squire's words, "The data clearly reveal that in most schools the classrooms are teacher-dominated." [1]

Because so many of our fellow English teachers know so little about current directions in the teaching of English and so little about their own performance in the classroom, I wish to urge supervisors to help teachers in the field discover themselves and their subject. I ask you to address yourselves to finding the means to inspire greater self-knowledge in English teachers at all levels and to reduce the incredible time lag between the generation of an idea or method in English and its successful implementation in the classroom.

It is perhaps astonishing to realize that the English profession had known very little about itself until the late 1960s. We have embossed our professional lives with opinions and studies and recommendations but with few hard facts. And without these facts about the teaching and learning of English at various levels, we have been unable to see our teaching in any perspective. James Squire's high school studies, Thomas Wilcox's *National Survey of Undergraduate English Programs,* Don Cameron Allen's study of *The Ph.D. in English and American Literature,* and the current MLA-NCTE *Study of Junior College English,* give us hard data about the education we have been providing for young people, data which cannot be ignored, no matter how painful it may occasionally be. Teachers and professors cannot, obviously, examine their own practices carefully if they do not know of these studies. One might argue that information and publications about them all have been readily available in professional journals and in the speeches and panels which dot our national conventions. Yet a great many—let us hope not a majority—of our teachers and professors are still uninformed and will likely remain uninformed in the next few years. Although the NCTE placed full-page advertisements in its journals urging teachers to read the reports on the Dartmouth Seminar of 1966 written by John Dixon and Herbert Muller if they read nothing else all year, only about 10,000 teachers purchased each volume. Ninety percent of our profession—perhaps

that uncomfortable figure is somewhat too high—still knows
little or nothing about that seminar, which was very likely the
most significant conference in English since the Basic Issues
Conference in 1958. We all know the reasons: the teacher's busy
schedule, high turnover in many of our schools, inertia, insecur-
ity, and incapacity. But we must be alarmed by the consequences
of this lack of knowledge: classrooms do not benefit from new
ideas, curriculum grows out-of-date, the intellectual vitality of a
faculty is vitiated. In very practical terms, teachers choose textbooks which contain badly abridged, irrelevant selections. They
teach school grammar because they once learned to the satisfaction of an older generation of teachers how to muddy the waters
of real grammar with arbitrary usages. They mark errors on
student papers with a vengeance and dedication which continues to inhibit young people from ever expressing themselves
freely. Worst of all, they drone on and on in class, sure that
they are communicating the great tradition, if only to eager
Johnny or bright Betsy, while the rest of the class dreams of the
real world and idles by until the bell brings an escape. It is a
situation which we cannot condone or even endure but which
we seem, somehow, powerless to correct without having the
time and chance to work with every English teacher at every
level one by one. Even the thousands of splendid teachers are
often so burdened with classes, with preparations, with student
conferences, and with extra-curricular responsibilities that they
cannot read and discuss the wealth of material on English which
is bringing real change to the English curriculum.

Some educators do not believe that we can meet the challenge. In a delightful new book, *Teaching as a Subversive Activity*, Neil Postman and Charles Weingartner argue that

> . . . within the "Educational Establishment" there are insufficient
> daring and vigorous ideas on which to build a new approach to
> education [2]

and that

> the fact is that our present educational system is not viable
> and is certainly not capable of generating enough energy to
> lead to its own revitalization.[3]

They offer sixteen rather extraordinary proposals: they would,
for example,

> Declare a five-year moratorium on the use of all textbooks
> Transfer all the elementary school teachers to high school and
> vice versa

Require every teacher who thinks he knows his "subject" well to write a book on it

Limit each teacher to three declarative sentences per class, and fifteen interrogatives

Prohibit teachers from asking any question they already know the answer to

Declare a moratorium on all tests and grades

Classify teachers according to their ability and make the lists public.[4]

I would be fully in agreement with almost all of their provocative, original ideas except for the requirement that more teachers write more books. We had, you may know, 90,000 papers in language and literature published last year. Because there is little chance that Messrs. Postman and Weingartner, for all their energy, will have their day, we must look to more practical ways of reaching and of changing English teachers and teaching.

Let me summarize briefly the current state of our predicament in the teaching of composition and then suggest what you as state consultants, directors, and supervisors can do to help teachers know, use, and, in some cases, avoid composition materials now available for the schools.

In the first flush of Project English, Richard Braddock and colleagues from the University of Iowa received funds to explore the state of our knowledge about composition. This important study, *Research in Written Composition,* surveyed more than 500 studies and projects and reported to the profession that all but a handful were largely a waste of time. Most apparent to Richard Braddock was the abysmal state of our knowledge about a subject taught throughout most of the school year and of obvious interest to every English teacher. He was, of course, able to single out a few studies of merit, including that by Roland Harris which warned "that the study of English grammatical terminology had a negligible or even a relatively harmful effect upon the corrections of children's writing. . . ."[5] The report further introduced two dozen subjects for future, carefully controlled research in composition, only a few of which have yet been undertaken.[6]

At about the same time, beginning in 1962, the major Curriculum Study Centers in English attacked the problem of composition. Was writing to be taught as a skill? Did calling composition "rhetoric" mean that one had to introduce the works of Quintilian, Richard Hurd, and Wayne Booth into the curriculum in order to give the course a "content"? Could a sequential, cumulative, spiral curriculum in composition be devised which could be carefully integrated into a total K-12 curriculum? The answers were various. Wallace Douglas at Northwestern chose to emphasize the process of writing, developed exercises which stressed the pre-writing stages, and urged teachers and students to be more interested in voice, audience, and content than in correctness or any given set of mechanics. Oregon taught transformational-generative grammar but carefully claimed no relationship between knowledge of this new grammar and improvement in writing ability. It stressed, rather, substance, structure, and style and worked toward a sequential composition program. Most daringly, Nebraska tried to integrate the study of language and rhetoric and produced units which must be judged very carefully, especially in the light of later claims for the efficacy of transform grammar in helping young people to write. Andrew Schiller developed lessons on revision for the ninth grade in which transformations are used as one of four principal kinds of revisions which will give the student command of a wide variety of sentence patterns and types. And Francis Christenson, working with Nebraska teachers, continued to develop his generative rhetoric of the sentence.

Before these materials had become widely known, except to the limited number of teachers who had attended NDEA institutes, two very different approaches to the teaching of composition were being hotly debated. On the one hand, if the research reported by Donald Bateman and Frank Zidonis in *The Effect of a Study of Transformational Grammar on the Writing of Ninth and Tenth Graders* [7] was valid, and I must note that serious reservations about their research techniques have been voiced, then teachers at last had a concrete way to improve student writing and to save the teaching of grammar at the same time. Many teachers automatically—and mistakenly—equated the results of the Zidonis and Bateman study with the goals of the transform grammar included in the Oregon package and with the use of transformations in the revision process at Nebraska. The millennium was at hand! But it was a millennium based on false or spotty information.

On the other hand, those attending the Dartmouth Seminar pleaded for more oral composition, for more creative work, for more opportunities for dramatic improvisation—especially at the expense of time formerly spent on the teaching of grammar or of usage. Unfortunately the Dartmouth Seminar was a closed meeting except to a small group of educators. Only after books and monographs about Dartmouth had begun to appear could teachers begin to consider the implications of the Seminar for the teaching of composition in their classrooms. Fortunately, two films on *Improvised Drama* (distributed by Peter Robeck and Company, Inc.) are now available to the classroom teacher. These films allow the teacher to watch the theories of John

Dixon and the Dartmouth Seminar being tested in the classroom, to examine closely alternatives to traditional ways of teaching, and, one hopes, to try them out in the classroom.

To my knowledge, only one piece of research has established "that some kind of formal language exercises can cause students to write with greater syntactic fluency than normal growth would occasion."[8] In his absorbing review of current trends in language study in *Teaching the Universe of Discourse*, James Moffett is at great pains to assess John Mellon's research properly:

> It is essential to be precise about what this valuable study proves: *embedding exercises* based on transformational rules will improve syntactic versatility in writing. It does not substantiate the hypothesis that instruction in transformational grammar will produce these results.[9]

Moffett also recommends other methods for developing syntactic maturity:

> Sentence-expansion games, good discussion, rewriting of notes, collaborative revision of compositions, playing with one-sentence discourses, and verbalizing certain cognitive tasks.[10]

While the debate about grammar and composition continues, the debate about the value of most language and composition workbooks seems settled except for the thousands of teachers and administrators who continue to buy them in the mistaken notion that they will help students to develop writing skills. James Lynch and Bertrand Evans, in *High School English Textbooks*, had too academic a view of English, but they did document carefully the deadly repetitiveness of language and composition books which were giving ". . . *essentially the same treatment [to each part of speech] in any volume of any particular series that is given in the other volumes of that series.*"[11] In 1968 Moffett summed up his dissatisfaction with composition books and writing texts from the more humanitarian approach to English associated with Dartmouth:

> They install in the classroom a mistaken and unwarranted method of learning. They take time, money, and energy that should be spent on authentic writing, reading, and speaking. They get between the teacher and his students, making it difficult for the teacher to understand what they need, and to play a role that would give them the full benefit of group process. . . . Because they predict and pre-package, they are

bound to be inappropriate for some school populations, partly irrelevant to individual students, and ill-timed for all.[12]

Moffett sees, rather, "the sequence of psychological development" as "the backbone of curriculum continuity" and believes that "logical formulations of the subject should serve only as an aid in describing this natural growth," [13] a position not so much at variance with the best units developed by the Study Centers as those who have attacked the "content curriculum" would claim. Jerome Bruner and Northrop Frye influenced the development of the Nebraska curriculum in composition as well as language and literature—but so did Jean Piaget, to whom Moffett also turns:

The primary dimension of growth seems to be a movement from the center of the self outward. Or perhaps it is more accurate to say that the self enlarges, assimilating the world to itself and accommodating itself to the world, as Piaget puts it. . . . In moving outward from himself, the child becomes more himself. The teacher's art is to move with this movement, a subtle act possible only if he shifts his gaze from the subject to the learner, for the subject is the learner.[14]

What then of composition? Wallace Douglas writes,

What would the teacher do if there were no students who committed errors, none whose work showed definite differences from the forms and styles of writing found in the literature anthologies that the teacher used in college?

He recommends that the English teacher "so far as conscience, schoolroom and parents will allow" let the child "alone to do his own experimenting with his own grammatical and stylistic patterns and transformations." [15]

Moffett advocates much the same technique:

The role of the teacher, then, is to teach the students to teach each other. This also makes possible a lot more writing and a lot more response to the writing than a teacher could otherwise sponsor. He creates cross-teaching by setting up two kinds of group processes—one that he leads with the whole class, and a smaller one that runs itself.[16]

At the same time that the best of our scholars and teachers are calling for greater freedom in the teaching of writing, the community has begun to take an ever closer look at the curriculum and to demand a voice in the selection of teachers and in curriculum planning. This growing voice often calls for skills—correct spelling, standard usage, the ability to write and punctuate a coherent paragraph—but it also demands that we extend our efforts to reach *every* child.

I could muddy the waters further by introducing the related questions of an appropriate language curriculum, a broadened base for the selection of literature for the schools, the introduction and impact of media, and the integration of all of the components of the English curriculum in the classroom. Let me, instead, sum up where we are and try to suggest the implications for you and for the classroom teacher. What do we know? (1) No one has proved the connection between the learning of any grammatical system and growth in the ability to write or to express oneself orally. If grammar is to be introduced into the curriculum at all, then, it should be introduced as a discipline in itself. (2) No textbook which makes claims about the effect of grammar on writing, therefore, can be trusted. Moreover, there is widespread feeling that workbooks with exercises have limited if any use in the English classroom. (3) Oral and creative activities which involve young people are as essential to the composition class as any written activities. Those studying composition, however, would agree that students should begin to write early and should write regularly. (4) Although usage and the mechanics of spelling and punctuation should play some part in the composition classroom, they must be *radically* de-emphasized. (5) Most important, English teachers desperately need information and ideas in order to free themselves from old practices, required textbooks, their own insecurities, and the uninformed displeasures of their colleagues, administrators, and communities. Inservice work is the key to the problem.

No one responsible for the education of teachers and the improvement of curriculum can forget other trends and innovations, but it seems to me that supervisors must focus on the few activities which affect each English teacher every week in almost every class. You must ordinarily concentrate on more plebeian matters, selecting perhaps one or two topics each year for analysis, synthesis, discussion, and recommendation and attempting to saturate your district or state with information about discrete parts of the curriculum. Obviously you will distribute newsletters with small, carefully annotated bibliographies and conduct local and regional workshops, but I should like to suggest four additional, specific ways to make the information you have at your disposal more useful to each school:

1. First, goad the consciences of the English department chair-

men in your secondary schools (and colleges, I might add). If you can move them, you can move the faculty and change the curriculum.

2. Second, whenever you hold a workshop or visit a school, invite—and try to force—the participation of an academician from a nearby teacher-training institution. Good pre-service work in composition will be developed by the college English departments, for example, only as individual faculty members learn about the school curriculum. College professors have the time and the resources to do research in composition if they become interested. I would be willing to wheedle, cajole, and exaggerate to some of them to get them into the schools. You must not here be determined to persuade the hard-working specialist in English Education. He is already committed. Go after the young scholar, especially the new associate professor. Invite him to speak at your workshop, to visit a school library, to attend or even teach class, to advise about a particular selection in a textbook which badly needs revision. You may arouse his interest and win his support.

3. Although the busy secondary teacher does not have time to keep fully abreast of recent developments in composition or in linguistics, you can stimulate his participation in both formal and informal in-service work in the school. Urge the chairman to have each member of his staff read in one particular area, try out some of the ideas he discovers, and report them to his colleagues. You can provide outside expertise and publicity, but when you leave the building, the curriculum stands still again unless the school is working regularly with the college and unless the English department in the school has agreed to carry on its reading, however piecemeal. To both groups—school and college—you can provide information about in-service programs for credit which have been given in the school itself. When a large number of faculty members from the same school study together, change comes far more quickly to the curriculum.

4. Finally, begin to work more closely with junior and community college teachers in your district or state. I believe that they need and want the kind of help with reading and composition that the state supervisor can offer. Bring them in as resource persons and let them, too, stay both to teach and to learn. In large urban areas, as community control of schools grows, the close cooperation of the schools and of the junior colleges will become even more important.

If the task seems overwhelming and the rewards tenuous at best, take comfort in the knowledge that you will have splendid opportunities to use your highest qualities—intelligence, knowledge, good humor, administrative ability—and your lowest—deviousness, trickery—all in a good cause.

1. James R. Squire, *A Study of English Programs in Selected High Schools Which Consistently Educate Outstanding Students in English.* Cooperative Research Report No. 1994 (1966), p. 97 and p. 105.

2. From *Teaching as a Subversive Activity,* by Neil Postman and Charles Weingartner. Copyright © 1969 by Neil Postman and Charles Weingartner. Reprinted by permission of the publisher, Delacorte Press. p. xiv.

3. Ibid., p. xv.

4. Ibid., pp. 137-140.

5. Richard Braddock, Richard Lloyd-Jones, and Lowell Schoer, *Research in Written Composition* (Urbana, Illinois: National Council of Teachers of English, 1963), p. 83.

6. Ibid., pp. 52-53.

7. Donald Bateman and Frank J. Zidonis, *The Effect of a Study of Transformational Grammar on the Writing of Ninth and Tenth Graders,* Research Report No. 6 (Urbana, Illinois: National Council of Teachers of English, 1966).

8. James Moffett, *Teaching the Universe of Discourse* (Boston: Houghton Mifflin Company, 1968), p. 166. Reprinted by permission of the publisher.

9. Ibid., p. 167.

10. Ibid., pp. 180-181.

11. James J. Lynch and Bertrand Evans, *High School English Textbooks* (Boston: Little, Brown and Company, 1963), p. 242.

12. Moffett, p. 209.

13. Ibid., p. 14.

14. Ibid., p. 59.

15. Wallace Douglas, "Introduction" to *Lessons in Composition for High School* (Evanston, Illinois: Northwestern Curriculum Study Center in English, 1967), p. 2 ff.

16. Moffett, p. 196.

*M. Shugrue*

# Bibliography

Barnes, Douglas, ed. *Drama in the English Classroom.* Urbana: NCTE, 1968. (ED 020 177: EDRS Price: MF-$0.50 HC—not available from EDRS; available from NCTE: Stock No. 36259, $1.50 65 pp.)

Barnes, Douglas and James Britton. *Language, the Learner and the School.* Includes a document prepared by the London Association for the Teaching of English with an introduction by Harold Rosen. Harmondsworth, Middlesex, England: Penquin, 1969. (Available from NCTE: Stock No. 22433, $1.25 128 pp.)

Barry, James D. "Implementing the Guidelines of the English Teacher Preparation Study," in *Revisiting Basic Issues in English Education:* Selected Papers and Addresses Delivered at the Sixth Conference on English Education, University of Colorado, March 28-30, 1968, Part I, edited by Oscar M. Haugh. Urbana: NCTE, 1968, pp. 13-18. (Available from NCTE: Stock No. 20578, $1.75 71 pp.)

Bell, Vicais. *On Learning the English Tongue.* London: Faber and Faber, 1953.

Blackburn, Thomas. *Presenting Poetry:* A Handbook for English Teachers. London: Methuen and Co., Ltd., 1966.

Britton, James, ed. *Talking and Writing:* A Handbook for English Teachers. London: Methuen and Co., Ltd., 1967.

Brown, Mary and Norman Precious. *The Integrated Day in the Primary School*. London: Ward Lock Educational Publishers, 1968.

Carrithers, Lura M. A review of Herbert J. Muller's *The Uses of English, Elementary English*, 45(May 1968): 656-57.

Clegg, A. B. *The Excitement of Writing*. London: Chatto and Windus, 1965. (Available from NCTE: Stock No. 22406, $2.25 138 pp.)

Coogan, Philippa. "English Usage." *Momentum* (February 1970): 34-38.

Cooper, Gertrude E. *The Place of Play in an Infant and Junior School*. London: National Froebel Foundation, 1968.

Cutforth, J. A. *English in the Primary School*. Oxford: Basil Blackwell, 1964.

Cutforth, J. A. and S. H. Battersby. *Children and Books*. Oxford: Basil Blackwell, 1967. (Also New York: Humanities Press, 1962.)

Creber, J. W. Patrick. "Redirection in the Teaching of English," in *Revisiting Basic Issues in English Education:* Selected Papers and Addresses Delivered at the Sixth Conference on English Education, University of Colorado, March 28-30, 1968, Part I, edited by Oscar M. Haugh. Urbana: NCTE, 1968, pp. 1-8. (Available from NCTE: Stock No. 20578, $1.75 71 pp.)

———. *Sense and Sensitivity:* The Philosophy and Practice of English Teaching. London: University of London Press, Ltd., 1965. (Available from NCTE: Stock No. 22807 Hardbound, $4.25; Stock No. 22816 Soft cover, $2.50 253 pp.)

DeMott, Benjamin. "Reading, Writing, Reality, Unreality." *Educational Record*, 48(Summer 1967): 197-205. (ED 015 945: EDRS Price: MF-$0.25 HC-$0.60, 10 pp. This article has been reproduced in Squire's *Response to Literature*, pp. 31-48.)

Dixon, John. *Growth through English:* A Report Based on the Dartmouth Seminar 1966. Reading, England: NATE, 1967. (Available from NCTE: Stock No. 02507, $1.50 121 pp.)

Dixon, John and Wayne O'Neil. "Conference Report: The Dartmouth Seminar." *Harvard Educational Review*, 39(Spring 1969): 357-72.

Eastman, Arthur E. "Trends in the Teaching of Literature," in *The Future of the English Curriculum*, edited by James D. Barry New York: MLA, 1967, pp. 4-11. (The entire collection of essays edited by Barry is available as ED 013 831: EDRS Price: MF-$0.25 HC-$2.30, 44 pp.)

Evertts, Eldonna L., ed. *Explorations in Children's Writing*. Urbana: NCTE, 1970. (Available from NCTE: Stock No. 30353, $2.50 122 pp.)

———. *Study Guide for Dartmouth Publications*. Urbana: NCTE, 1969. (ED 032 308: EDRS Price: MF-$0.25 HC-$2.50, 48 pp.)

———. *What's New in Language Arts:* Composition. EKNE Elementary Instructional Service. Washington, D.C.: National Educational Association. (Available from NEA, Stock No. 282-08864, 8 pp.)

Eyre, Wallace. *Let's Imagine.* Oxford: Basil Blackwell, 1968.

Harris, Peter, ed., "Drama in Education." *English in Education* (1967): 72 pp. (Available from NCTE: Stock No. 22255, $1.75 72 pp.)

Heathcote, Dorothy. "How Does Drama Serve Thinking, Talking, and Writing?" *Elementary English,* 47(December 1970): 1077-1081.

Holbrook, David. *English for Maturity.* New York: Cambridge University Press, 1967.

———. *English for the Rejected:* Training Literacy in Lower Streams of the Secondary School. New York: Cambridge University Press, 1964.

———. *The Secret Places:* Essays on Imaginative Work in English Teaching and on the Culture of the Child. London: Methuen and Co., Ltd., 1964.

Jennings, F. G. A review of H. J. Muller's *The Uses of English. Saturday Review,* 50(December 16, 1967): 73.

Langdon, Margaret. *Let the Children Write:* An Explanation of Intensive Writing. London: Longmans, Green and Co., 1966. (Available from NCTE: Stock No. 22451, $1.00 72 pp.)

Lewis, E. Glyn. "Postscript to Dartmouth—or Poles Apart." *College English,* 29(March 1968): 426-434.

Marckwardt, Albert H. "From the Basic Issues Conference to the Dartmouth Seminar: Perspectives on the Teaching of English." An address given at a meeting of the NCTE College Section Committee, December 1966. *PMLA,* 82(September 1967): 8-13. (ED 016 683: EDRS Price: MF-$0.25 HC-$0.45, 7 pp.)

———. "The Dartmouth Conference in Retrospect." *English Quarterly,* 3(Spring 1970): 7-19.

———. "The Dartmouth Seminar." *NASSP Bulletin,* 51(April 1967): 101-106.

———. *Language and Language Learning.* Urbana: NCTE, 1968. (ED 026 360: EDRS Price: MF-$0.50 HC—not available from EDRS; available from NCTE: Stock No. 25653, $1.50 81 pp.)

———. "The Other Side of the Coin." *College English,* 28(February 1967): 383-388.

Marshall, Sybil. *Adventure in Creative Education.* Oxford: Pergamon Press, Ltd., 1968.

———. *An Experiment in Education.* Cambridge, England: Cambridge University Press, 1966.

Matthews, Dorothy. "The Teaching of Drama in High School." *Illinois English Bulletin* (1969). (Available from NCTE: Stock No. 38499, $0.35 20 pp.)

Moffett, James. *Drama—What is Happening:* The Use of Dramatic Activities in the Teaching of English. Urbana: NCTE, 1967. (ED 017 505: EDRS Price: MF-$0.50 HC—not available from EDRS. Available from NCTE: Stock No. 17751, $1.25 62 pp. This is reprinted in Moffett's *Teaching the Universe of Discourse,* pp. 60-119. See below.)

———. *A Student-Centered Language Arts Curriculum, Grades K-13:*

A Handbook for Teachers. Boston: Houghton Mifflin, 1968. (Available from publisher, $7.25 503 pp.)

————. *Teaching the Universe of Discourse.* Boston: Houghton Mifflin, 1968. (Available from publisher, $2.75 Paperbound 215 pp.)

Muller, Herbert J. *The Uses of English:* Guidelines for the Teaching of English from the Anglo-American Conference at Dartmouth College. New York: Holt, Rinehart, Winston, Inc., 1967. (Available from NCTE: Stock No. 05309, $2.95 176 pp.)

Muskopf, Allan and Joy Moss. "An Integrated Day Workshop." *The Elementary School Journal,* 71(March 1971): 315-319.

National Association for the Teaching of English. *English in the Primary School:* Being the Evidence of the Association Presented to the Plowden Committee, 1964. (Available from NCTE: Stock No. 22308, $1.00 30 pp.)

————. *Poetry.* NATE Bulletin 3(Spring 1966) (Available from NCTE: Stock No. 22709, $1.50 56 pp.)

————. *Primary English.* NATE Bulletin 4(Autumn 1966) (Available from NCTE: Stock No. 22754, $2.00 84 pp.)

————. *Some Aspects of Oracy.* NATE Bulletin 2(Summer 1965) (Available from NCTE: Stock No. 22905, $1.00 44 pp.)

————. "Writing." *English in Education,* 3(Autumn 1969) (Available from NCTE: Stock No. 23192, $1.75 128 pp.)

Nevi, Charles N. "*Growth through English:* Another Appraisal." *English Journal,* 58(September 1969): 912-919.

Olson, Paul A., ed. *The Uses of Myth.* Urbana: NCTE, 1968. (Available from NCTE: Stock No. 39407, $1.50 61 pp.)

Quirk, Randolph. *The Use of English.* New York: St. Martin's Press, 1968.

Ridgway, Lorna and Irene Lawton. *Family Grouping in the Infant's School.* London: Ward Lock Educational Publishers, 1965.

Rogers, Vincent R. *Teaching in the British Primary School.* New York: The Macmillan Co., 1970.

Rogers, Vincent R. and Clarence R. Calder. "The British Primary School: Photo Essay." *Phi Delta Kappan,* 52(March 1971): 421-424.

Shugrue, Michael F. "The Lessons of Dartmouth," in the author's *English in a Decade of Change.* New York: Pegasus, 1968, pp. 73-78. (Book available from NCTE: Stock No. 01955, $1.95: NCTE members $1.75 204 pp.)

Squire, James R., ed. *A Common Purpose:* The Teaching of English in Great Britain, Canada, and the United States. Urbana: NCTE, 1966. (Stock No. 01107, $3.00 243 pp.)

————. "International Perspective on the Teaching of English." An address delivered at the opening of the general session of the International Conference on the Teaching of English, Vancouver, B.C., August 1967. *College English,* 29(March 1968): 419-425.

————. "The Running Water and the Standing Stone." An address given at the MLA General Meeting on English, Chicago, December 1967. *PMLA,* 83(June 1968): 523-529. (ED 024 672:

EDRS Price: MF-$0.25 HC-$0.50; reprints available from NCTE: Stock No. 10053, 10/$2.00 8 pp.)

———. *Response to Literature*. Urbana: NCTE, 1968. (ED 026 350: EDRS Price: MF-$0.50 HC—not available from EDRS; available from NCTE: Stock No. 37855, $1.50 86 pp.)

Squire, James R., and Roger K. Applebee. *Teaching English in the United Kingdom*. Urbana: NCTE, 1969. (Available from NCTE: Stock No. 05050, $3.25, 290 pp.)

Summerfield, Geoffrey, ed. *Creativity in English*. Urbana: NCTE, 1968. (ED 021 831: EDRS Price: MF-$0.50 HC—not available from EDRS; available from NCTE: Stock No. 01214, $1.50 76 pp.)

———. *Topics in English for the Secondary School*. London: B. T. Batsford, Ltd., 1965.

Walsh, J. H. *Teaching English:* To Children of Eleven to Sixteen, an Account of Day-to-Day Practice. London: Heinemann Educational Books, Ltd., 1965.

Watts, A. F. *The Language and Mental Development of Children:* An Essay on Educational Psychology. London: George G. Harrop and Co., 1944, 1966. (Available from NCTE: Stock No. 50508, $2.50 354 pp.)

Whitehead, Frank. *The Disappearing Dais:* A Story of the Principles and Practices of English Teaching. London: Chatto and Windus, 1966. (Available from NCTE: Stock No. 22200, $3.50 268 pp.)

Wilkinson, Andrew. "Oracy in English Teaching." *Elementary English*, 45(October 1968): 743-747.

———. *Spoken English*. Edgbaston, Birmingham, England: University of Birmingham, 1965. (Available from NCTE: Stock No. 23003, $2.25 131 pp.)

———. "The State of Language." *Educational Review* (1969) (Available from NCTE: Stock No. 23058, $2.25 128 pp.)

Winstanley, Barbara R. *Children and Museums*. Oxford: Basil Blackwell, 1967.

## ORDERING INFORMATION

### NCTE Ordering Information

The items in this bibliography which are designated "Available from NCTE" may be ordered by stock number from: National Council of Teachers of English, Order Department, 1111 Kenyon Road, Urbana, Illinois, 61801. Orders of less than $1.00 should be accompanied by remittance; add $0.40 handling charge to billed orders, regardless of amount.

### ERIC Document Ordering Information

The items in this bibliography which are available from the ERIC Document Reproduction Service (EDRS) have been assigned ED numbers and their entries contain EDRS prices. *Only* items with ED numbers can be ordered from EDRS.

EDRS reproduces documents in two ways: on microfiche (MF), a 4" × 6" microfilm card displaying up to 60 pages of text in micro-image; and hard copy (HC), a photographically-reproduced paper booklet. All orders must be in writing and must stipulate which kind is desired and the number of copies.

*PRICE CHANGE*: EDRS prices quoted in this bibliography do *not* reflect recent price changes. Effective March 1, 1971, any document ordered in microfiche reproduction costs only 65¢, regardless of the number of microfiche needed to reproduce the entire text of the document. Hard copy reproductions of ERIC documents are priced at $3.29 for every 100 pages of text in the original document.

170     Address orders for document reproductions to: ERIC Document Reproduction Service, P.O. Drawer 0, Bethesda, Maryland 20014. Payment must accompany orders under $10.00; no stamps or COD. Add sales tax or submit tax exemption certificate, if applicable. Book Rate or Library Rate postage is included in EDRS prices. The difference between Book Rate or Library Rate and First Class or Foreign Postage (outside the continental United States) rates will be billed at cost.

NOTE: Address all orders for ED-numbered documents to EDRS— NCTE/ERIC cannot fill orders for MF or HC.